BONUS OFFER

Because the topic in this book is so important to your ability to fulfill the call of God on your life; I want to make sure that you have all that you need to fulfill that call. Since my first books came out in 2000, I have traveled to over 50 nations carrying the important message of God@Work. This new book, God@Rest is a continuation of that message.

Because of that exposure, and more recently because of the TV program I host on GodTV; I have a large team of experts who can answer almost any need or question that you might have. In particular, I have teamed up with a powerfully successful marketplace prophet; not just one who prophesies, but one who can actually help you to fulfill the prophetic words spoken over you. Also on this team, is one of America's most effective business coaches who regularly sees zeros added to the bottom line of his client's income. Those two, along with me, bring the Biblical picture of the prophet, priest and king in a comprehensive consulting/coaching arrangement.

One of my passions is speaking to groups of business leaders who want to make a difference in the world. I can come to your corporation, association, group or church. Contact me at rich@Godisworking.com

Or if you are interested in acceleration of your business and impact; and your budget can handle it, contact me about the three of us working with your business on an annual contract.

I look forward to hearing from you.

God bless you as you find peace of mind in the middle of the battles you face.

Rich Marshall

GOD@ REST

THE KEYS TO PEACE OF MIND

GOD@ REST

THE KEYS TO PEACE OF MIND

Rich Marshall

God@Rest
THE KEYS TO PEACE OF MIND
By Rich Marshall
Copyright © 2018 by Rich Marshall

Printed in the United States of America

ISBN # 9781726224130

ENDORSEMENTS FOR GOD@REST

"In my experience working with high achievers, I have discovered that although most have traveled the globe, few have ever found life's most exclusive resort on earth - God's Rest. Let my friend Rich Marshall help you discover this special place and enjoy its bountiful blessings."

MELVIN PILLAY
Best Selling Author: *"The Power of Eight"*
President and Founder,
The Melchizedek Alliance

"Inside the pages of this book lie the secrets to more peace, happiness, and (indeed) rest. If you want to change the world, but still don't know how, then get ready because this book is for you! Rich Marshall is a "Top Gun" at showing you how to live with more abundance, joy, and results. Read this book now and enjoy!"

ED RUSH
5-Time #1 Best Selling Author
Former F-18 Fighter Pilot

"Rich Marshall is a gift from God to the body of Christ around the world. He is a prolific writer and an amazing teacher. His book, God@Work made a distinct impact of my life and changed my thinking forever. Rich has now written an important follow-up book: God@Rest, where he clearly lays out for you how to receive supernatural peace of mind through God's power and presence during these difficult and turbulent days. God@Rest will keep you motivated in the days when your mind is bombarded with negativity and will get you back on the path to fulfilling the call of God in your life."

WARD SIMPSON
President and CEO-God TV

ACKNOWLEDGMENTS

There are a number of people who contributed in powerful ways that have allowed me to finish this book project; and I want to thank them right now.

My wife of over 50 years is my rock, my prayer partner and chief intercessor; Wilma, without you this book would be just a thought in my mind. Thank you for always encouraging me to pursue those God ordained plans! Along with Father God, the Lord Jesus and the Holy Spirit, you have been my motivation and key supporter for writing this book. Could not do it without you!

There are many who have encouraged me along the way; far too many to mention by name. However, there are some that have been hands on and I want to give a shout out to these. Ken Walker has been my editor and writing consultant. When Ken and I are in "writing mode" it is an exciting journey. Thank you Ken. Bobbie Stedman is a meticulous proof reader, and made sure that most (if not all) of the typos etc. were corrected. She also added valuable input regarding content and layout. Thank you Bobbie, and also to Bob Stedman who was brought in as Bobbie and I worked on this together. And what one set of eyes might miss, another will see; and that was the case with my other proof reader; Velma

X | GOD@REST: THE KEYS TO PEACE OF MIND

Hoffer. Velma is a voracious reader and a good friend who added her expertise in this final version. Thank you Velma.

I want to thank Tamara Parsons at kentype.com for the beautiful formatting job she has done. Thank you Tamara. The cover design was done by 99Designs, where I had over 40 entries in a contest to choose a cover.

My family, especially our children and their families, are a great source of encouragement and support. I love you all: son Rich and Cece along with three of my precious grandkids; Spencer, Annalise and Keira. Daughter Valerie and her husband Joe; and three more of my precious grandkids; Skyler, Haylee, and Cassidy. I love each of you!

TABLE OF CONTENTS

GOD@REST
INTRODUCTION

I f you are one of those who really wants some peace of mind, and you are tired of rules, regulations, or "to do" lists; this is for you. So please, do yourself a favor and look at the templates, outlines, and prayers as examples instead of as another set of directives that you *must* follow. That said, the ideas presented here are powerful and will work for you if you use them. Just do so in a spirit of joyful cooperation with God, not as trying to follow a legalistic set of obligations.

I am very excited about this book! It has been on my heart for years; as it deals with issues that I am very familiar with. God@Rest does not just confront themes that I have read about or seen at a distance. This deals with things that I have had to deal with personally.

First of all; let me address what this book is NOT about. The rest that I am speaking of does not have anything to do with getting more sleep. Even though we should probably all get more sleep. In fact I just read in Health.com: *"Sleep makes you feel better, but its importance goes way beyond just boosting your mood or banishing under-eye circles. Adequate sleep is a key part of a healthy lifestyle, and can benefit your heart, weight, mind, and more."*

Good information; but not my point.

God@Rest is also not about taking time off, working less hours or going on a vacation. Again; not a bad idea. An article in Forbes Magazine in February of 2104 points out this interesting fact: *"Not taking vacation time is a bad idea, as it harms productivity and the economy. Those are key findings of a new study released earlier this month."[1]*

 Again, good information; but not my point.

Also, I should add; God@Rest has nothing to do with God taking a rest. First of all, He does not need to, because as the Bible tells us "He finished His work from the foundations of the world". (Hebrews 4:3) And even though He finished His work, in the sense that He has already completed all that is needed for both our salvation and for us to fulfill our God-given purpose, the all-powerful God is at work for us right now; and He does not need a break.

Ok; so God@Rest is not about sleep, vacations, or working less. Instead, this book is all about a state of mind. When the Hebrews writer referred to this "rest"; he said some will enter it and some will not. (Hebrews 4:1 "Therefore, since a promise remains of entering His rest, let us fear lest any of you seem to have come short of it.") This rest is attained through faith and is missed by lack of faith. In other words, it has nothing to do with sleep or time off. When Jesus speaks of "rest", He says it is "rest for your souls". (Matthew 11:29) As I will address later; your soul speaks of your mind. So Jesus is actually offering you peace of mind! And not only offering; but also showing you how to attain what He is ready to give to you!

And that is what I am speaking about; rest for your mind, real peace of mind. Those things that keep you from sleep because you can't shut down your thoughts. The things that keep you from focusing because the mind is racing off in directions that have nothing to do with your current focus or activity. I am talking to one whose mind is always active, but not always productively active.

I want to speak to your mind; because that is where Jesus promises "rest". I want to help bring you to that place, where the mind full of worries, stress and fear can instead come to a place of rest in God. Do you need this message? I sure do. And many people that I know do too. If your mind just took off on a tangent when I mentioned worry, stress and fear; then you need it also.

So, come with me on this journey of finding the keys to peace of mind.

(If you did not read the introduction; go back and read it now. It lays a good foundation for what the book is about and what it is not about. Reading the introduction will help you grasp the intent of this book quickly.)

CHAPTER 1
FINDING A LASTING REST

"Come to Me,.....I will give you rest."

~ Matthew 11:28

One afternoon, I was riding my bicycle on a familiar road. As a larger-than-normal bike rider, I could navigate level surfaces relatively quickly, and I could really fly downhill. Uphill climbs were a whole other story. One day on a particular climb (not that steep but long) the pavement seemed to stretch out for miles. I approached the hill with certainty that I would struggle, go slow, and reach the point of exhaustion by the time I made it to the top. Since I hadn't started riding bikes until I was fifty years old, I routinely experienced exhaustion.

However, this day as I started up the hill I didn't experience any decrease in speed. I even had to glance back to make sure I was going uphill. Sure enough, as I climbed higher and higher I maintained the pace. The further I went, the more exhilarated I felt. I finally broke into a shout of praise! Excited would be an understatement. It felt like my entire bike riding experience had reached a higher level. I could climb with the best of them.

Then I realized the source of my sudden uphill acceleration: a tailwind. My strength, my abilities, and my hill-climbing expertise had not changed one iota. The wind had shifted and was literally blowing me along. When I didn't have to rely on my own strength, it made hill climbing easy. So it is with the Lord. Let Jesus be the wind at your back! He makes it easy. That day, I did not need extra training. I simply needed to be in the right place at the right time. Position yourself, your mind, your attitude, and your very existence right in the yoke with Jesus. He will carry you through! It is easy because the wind of the Spirit is with you!

It is that power from God to keep you on track, to quiet the doubts in your mind, to help you experience real peace that this book is all about. That is what the rest of God is! In life, some people find the life-giving, energy-giving rest that God has promised. Others, with the same opportunities and options, end up full of negativism and irritability; no rest and no peace of mind. *God@Rest* is the long-awaited follow-up to my first two books. Released at the dawn of the marketplace ministry movement, *God@Work* and *God@Work* Volume 2 (which I will refer to as *God@Work II*) brought needed messages to the body of Christ. God used them in a powerful, life-changing way for many of God's frontline— but often overlooked—marketplace ministers. Since the first book's release in 2000, a worldwide movement of these ministers emerged, most recently stimulating the creation of the "Seven Mountains" movement. Often criticized and mischaracterized, in reality this movement simply encourages believers in Christ to bring God's influence and standards into worldly venues instead of being content to express them solely in a church setting.

If you are one of those marketplace ministers called by God and described in *God@Work II*, you either need, or soon will need, the message of *God@Rest*. I have recognized this need, at least conceptually, for many years. At one of our earliest marketplace ministry conferences, Sam Benson—a longtime pastor and now a ministry overseer at Destiny Christian Church in Burnsville, Minnesota—preached a message from Hebrews 4. The chapter begins: "Therefore, since a promise remains of entering His rest, let us fear lest any of you seem to have come short of it. For indeed the gospel was preached to us as well as to them; but the word which they heard did not profit them, not being mixed with faith in those who heard it" (Heb. 4:1-2).

Benson's message focused on the promise of rest the Lord has given His children. I picked up on his words and have been seeking, studying and trying to understand this rest since then. A few years ago, prolific author and Prophet James Goll turned to me in a conference where we were both speaking and remarked: "Your next book will be titled 'God@ Rest.' " I responded: "Wow! That sounds like God to me." And it was! However, it took me years to learn some lessons and enter into this rest fully enough to share it with you.

Let me illustrate with the story of two men: Robert and Ted. They lived in seemingly parallel worlds. Both held the same advanced business degree, which helped them maneuver their way through high-pressure, fast-moving worlds. Both occupied positions made tougher by the turbulent twenty-first century economy. They even followed the same daily routine: up at the crack of dawn and out the door to beat rush-hour traffic to the office. There they worked non-stop throughout the day before turning out the lights.

As you can imagine, both achieved worldly success. They ascended the corporate ladder at an accelerated pace, earning regular promotions and generous salary increases. Between their smoothly-functioning organizations and well-manicured suburban homes and loving families, they seemed to possess everything they needed to make them happy.

In addition to these business and personal achievements, their respective walks of faith, at least to those looking on; mirrored each other as well. Both were Christians and regular church attenders and others looked at them as leaders in the faith community. They often expressed their beliefs to co-workers, despite the perils that exist for anyone daring to "proselytize" in the modern workplace. They knew the Bible well, could quote scripture, and routinely applied Christian principles to the daily news. Interpreting the headlines, they reviewed current events and explained the parallels to Scripture. Namely, how following biblical patterns brings success, while ignoring them reaps disaster. They had no doubt that their work was God's plan for their lives; it represented a primary motivation for their daily existence. They knew that God had called them to work as their ministry and mission field.

Robert and Ted were so successful and powerful, many of their friends could have easily envied their rapid climbs toward the top. Yet, at the end of each day, a mammoth gulf existed between these two, apparently indistinguishable executives. At first, others could hardly discern the difference. Over time, it grew until it became obvious to anyone who took the time to examine the situation.

Robert remained optimistic, energized, and excited about the future. He peppered his daily conversation with talk of expansion, growth, and making an impact for the kingdom of God. Robert's outward focus surfaced through his plans to provide better care for his employees, including the addition of a corporate chaplain to serve the needs of his staff. You see; Robert had learned to enter into the rest of God in the midst of the storms that life might send his way.

He had learned to let God handle the stress and he had complete peace of mind. Hebrews 4:10 would describe him in this way: "For he who has entered His rest has himself also ceased from his works as God did from His."

Ted, on the other hand, began to show signs of weariness. He was becoming increasingly irritable; and he even expressed skepticism toward any suggestions of expansion or growth. While the normally upbeat leader became more and more negative, the atmosphere around him—whether in the office or at home—took on the same negative and somber feel. Ted had not learned how to enter into the energy producing and life giving power of "God's rest." As a result, the Bible describes him with these strong words in Hebrews 3:12: "Beware, brethren, lest there be in any of you an evil heart of unbelief in departing from the living God." Sound too strong? That is how the Hebrews writer describes this rest: Faith is the doorway to rest; if you want real peace of mind, faith is the ticket! On the other hand, and I know this sounds harsh, unbelief, in fact "the evil heart of unbelief" is the obstacle that will keep you from His rest. While faith is the ticket to peace of mind, lack of faith will cause you undue stress and an unrelenting troubled mind. Like Robert and Ted, you have choices to make. Not necessarily hard choices; but faith choices.

And so it goes with the story of Robert and Ted, while both looked alike on the outside, the key difference between them existed on the inside: only one of these two executives knew how to enter the rest of God. Namely, finding Him in every situation so he could draw strength from His presence! You see, the rest to which I am referring is not fulfilled by taking a day off or going on a long vacation. While everyone needs breaks, I am talking about the strength derived from walking in the center of God's will. This will provide the resolve and inner peace that comes from knowing He is the wind at your back in what might otherwise be an incredibly stressful situation. There are answers for all of us in this kind of ongoing, refreshing rest. In the pages ahead, I invite you to learn more about this satisfying solution to life's dilemmas, problems, and fears.

CHAPTER 2
ENTERING GOD'S REST
(OR, "WATERSLIDE CHRISTIANITY")

*Therefore, since a promise remains of
entering His rest, let us fear lest any of you
seem to have come short of it.*

~ Hebrews 4:1

The island nation of Haiti has seen so many earthquakes it seems to sit on the Caribbean version of the San Andreas Fault. Typhoons, hurricanes, flooding, infectious diseases, and death are part of this scenario of misery. This continuing cavalcade of destruction propelled me into its midst shortly after one of its deadliest earthquakes. The mid-January 2010 disaster killed more than two hundred and thirty thousand and injured another three hundred thousand.

My eyes widened as the flight descended into Port-au-Prince, epicenter of the deadly quake. It looked like a bomb had exploded; hillsides were littered with rubble that had been houses just a few weeks before. As we landed and began driving through the streets, I was stunned to see men with wheelbarrows carrying the rubble to trucks. This would have been a herculean task with bull dozers and front-end loaders, but wheelbarrows and shovels made the task look impossible. And in fact, months and years later, the cleanup remained unfinished.

At the time, I was working as a corporate trainer, specializing in ethics and core values for an energy company based in the Caribbean. I was scheduled to be in Haiti just a couple of weeks after the earthquake for the training I was providing for the company. As a result of the earthquake, that trip was postponed and instead, I was asked to put my pastoral experience to work instead. The need was for someone to help staff members deal with the ongoing psychological issues that arose amid the trauma surrounding the earthquake. The 7.3 magnitude quake caused some eight billion dollars in damage and caused more than six hundred thousand people to flee to the safety of family members or friends living outside the capital. Seven years later, fifty-five thousand of these folks were still living in makeshift camps.[1]

Throughout my career as a pastor, I have been involved in some fashion or another with many catastrophes of various kinds. We experienced earthquakes large and small in California; I led a team to minister to the hurting after the Oklahoma City bombing; I had even traveled to Afghanistan back in 2002 during their time of rebuilding after the 9/11 terrorist attacks. So when the call came for a counselor to help with the staff in Haiti, the company commissioned me for the task.

On the flight into Haiti I prayed and asked God to help me. Indeed, I felt thoroughly inadequate to deal with this level of trauma, even though I had years of experience counseling people after all kinds of disasters. Have you ever felt like you were in over your head? I sure did this time; this one couldn't be managed through past experience or current knowledge. I knew that I needed to hear from the Lord—big time! As I prayed, something happened that shouldn't happen to "seriously spiritual people" in the middle of prayer: I fell asleep.

Although I don't recall being asleep for more than a few minutes, in that brief span of time I had a dream. In it, God showed me a large ant hill. As I looked at the hill, someone stepped on it, kicked it, and generally wreaked havoc. As I watched this battering unfold, many of the ants scattered. Yet, just as quickly most initiated the process of rebuilding the ant hill. Even before the devastation had ended, and surely before the ants' general could put a rebuilding plan in place, the ants were back at work to restore that crushed spectacle.

ANT-DRIVEN RESPONSE

As I awoke from that short nap and even shorter dream, I asked the Lord what this all meant. He replied, "Consider the ant." With my Bible in hand, I quickly located the reference in Proverbs: "Go to the ant, you sluggard! Consider her ways and be wise, which, having no captain, overseer or ruler, provides her supplies in the summer, and gathers her food in the harvest" (Prov. 6:6-8). Wow! What a prescription for an efficient disaster relief response. Without a captain, overseer, or ruler, the ant knows what to do. When disaster strikes, the ant goes to work.

I knew immediately the Lord was teaching me a lesson I could put to use that very day. Although I flew in several weeks after the earthquake occurred, some of the company's employees had not yet returned to work. Once I landed, I started looking for those who came back soon after the quake. I knew they were like the proverbial ant. These people wouldn't need a job assignment; they would know what to do simply because it needed to be done. They either were, or would become, great leaders in the company.

Considering the daunting nature of this assignment, I then asked, "What is the major issue I will be dealing with, Lord?" He replied with a one-word answer: "Fear." I saw that confirmed with every person I met in the days and weeks to follow. One after another spoke of fear: trepidations about another quake striking the island, fear of unstable buildings that might not hold up amid aftershocks, concern for their children, worries over their job future . . . the list was endless. It could be summarized as fear, fear, and more fear.

Ironically, this apprehension and anxiety brought me a strange sense of relief. Why? Because I knew how to deal with fear. The Bible makes it clear that the antidote for fear is love. Equipped with biblical insight, I told worker after worker: "The answer to your fear is love. Love for God, love for your family, love for your country, and love for your job." The same is true even when you're not in the midst of calamity. When you understand the love of God and fully embrace it, it will drive the rest of your life.

Many of these folks were having a hard time with the idea of returning to work. Recognizing this, I dealt with them on the basis of love. My advice can be summed up: When you love your family, you want to provide for them. How do you do that? You go to work and work as unto the Lord. Your family has certain needs that are met when you go to work. Love of family and love of work should fit together like a hand-and-glove. Plus, when you love your country, you want to help rebuild it. How do you do that? You go to work and help your company provide the needed services to help rebuild and strengthen your nation.

When you love God, you want to obey Him and work hard. Work appears early in the first book of the Bible. After the Lord worked to create the heavens and the earth, and everything on the earth, He told Adam and Eve: "Be fruitful and multiply; fill the earth and subdue it; have dominion over the fish of the sea, over the birds of the air, and over every living thing that moves on the earth" (Gen. 1:28). Love for God and love for work fit together.

RESTING DURING WORK

Despite these encouraging words, you may be wondering if it's possible to find "rest" in a situation like this. Is there rest when the world you have known comes crumbling down around you? Is there rest when the economy fails, and housing prices plummet, and looking for a job is about as exciting as a trip to the dentist. (Sorry Doctor.) Is there rest when you can no longer pay your bills? Is there rest when you are in danger of losing your home, your business, and everything materially that you have held dear? How can you find rest in the midst of upheaval and crippling dread?

Let's start by considering what this "rest" is, and what it is not. It is clear from Hebrews 4 that there is a divinely-orchestrated rest. It is also clear that some will enter it, and some will not. So, we know that it is possible to find this place of rest, just as we know it is also possible to miss it.

Rest can be defined in these ways:
1. Cease from action
2. Free from worry
3. Be settled

4. Be secure

5. Have something to lean on

All but the first item on the list (cease from action) are the most significant and practical because they identify what we really need. That's because the rest that I am referring to has nothing to do with ceasing action. In fact, as you rest in God, you may work harder than ever, and yet not feel exhausted or stressed out about it. It is possible to be free from worry, feel settled, and know the assurance of security because you have something to lean on.

That first meaning, "cease from action," can be confusing, because in the context of God's rest, resting does not mean ceasing from action. Instead, we are to be intimately involved in God's action. When you are simply doing things for the sake of busyness, or because you think it is the thing to do, you will soon get bogged down. That is when the pressure starts to build, and the results you expected never materialize. This is when doubt, fear, discouragement, and—ultimately—despair, begin to set in.

In the case of the workers in Haiti, some did simply "cease from action." They were so traumatized they could not even return to work. Other ant-like employees returned to work almost immediately.

However, even when ambitiously tackling the task at hand, God's marketplace leaders face a great temptation: to get so wrapped up in the task, and so sold out to the work itself, that we forget God and overlook His sovereignty. While we wouldn't consciously acknowledge this, it's like saying, "Thanks, Lord, for calling me. I'm so grateful to know that work is from You, and I know I can be a minister for You . . . so now I'll do it on my own. By the way, God, I'll call on you if I need any help along the way." Of course none of us would be so blatant as to put it that way. Still, that's the ultimate result. While we may be sold out to God's call, we try to complete the task in our own strength. Working with human understanding, we equate busyness with obedience, a full calendar with a call and purpose, and hard work for God-directed work.

RELYING ON GOD

Don't get me wrong, I believe in hard work; the Bible speaks of it in Genesis and many other places. Remember the Proverbs passage about the ant I referred to earlier? In addition to the challenge to remember the ant who works hard without being told what to do, Solomon adds: "A little sleep, a little slumber, a little folding of the hands to sleep—so shall poverty come on you like a prowler, and your need like an armed man" (Prov. 6:10-11). Then there is Paul's admonition: "If anyone will not work, neither shall he eat" (2 Thess. 3:10). Work is a mandate from God; it is a commandment that none of us can ignore.

We all know that the devil loves to counterfeit God's authentic activity. So, whenever God gives advice, commands, or instructions meant to benefit us, the enemy will produce a counterfeit shortcut that seems okay, but ultimately does not bring pleasing results. When it comes to our work, if the devil can get us to go to extremes and work so hard we forget God in the midst of it, he can gain the upper hand. I believe in today's high-stress, high-pressure world, this is happening all too often to many believers. Work becomes an effort of the flesh instead of a consistent and regular process of staying in touch with the Lord. When you complete your work in the flesh, exhaustion and eventually illness are likely to follow. When you do your work in cooperation with God, it leads to a rest that brings renewed energy and peace of mind.

An easy test to determine whether you are in the "rest of God" is to consider how you feel after a long, hard day. Are you worn out, on edge, angry at the world, and snapping at your family or others around you? Or are you energized, excited, and full of anticipation about tomorrow? When you find yourself on God's path, doing what He is calling for you to do, and doing it in His strength, it releases tremendous power. You may feel physically tired and at the same time be emotionally and spiritually energized.

This is what I discovered with a small group of Haitians. They were at peace in the middle of one of the world's greatest tragedies. They found rest by following a biblical principle: Get involved with what God is doing and find rest. In Haiti, one of the employees told me, "My truck was destroyed in the earthquake, so I have been walking to work." In fact, he was back on the job the same day, cleaning rubble and preparing to reopen the business as soon as possible. Others were not back to work yet when I went there again several weeks later.

SLIDING TO FREEDOM

I remember the time when our family visited a large water park. The mere appearance of the vast cornucopia of waterslides and other activities made the kids so excited they wanted to do everything at once. Our grandson was about two at the time and wanted to go down the largest waterslide of them all. Plus, he wanted to do it by himself. Followed by his father, he trudged to the top. Even though it looked much higher and more challenging from way up on high, he started down.

However, he was so light that he couldn't maintain any momentum. Just when he slipped out of sight around one of the sharp turns, the little fellow stopped dead in his tracks. There he sat in the middle of the waterslide, immobilized. This happened as Dad catapulted along behind him at full speed. As he rounded that bend in the slide, there sat his son. It was too late to slow down, much less stop! There was no room to get around the boy, either. So Dad did the only thing he could: reach out his arms, sweep his son into his lap, and safely carry him at full speed to the bottom.

I sometimes say that entering God's rest can be called "waterslide Christianity." We get excited about the heights, the thrill of the ride, and unseen and unexpected turns, only to realize we don't have enough "weight" to carry us all the way. Those who are successful in work as ministry are usually those who have chosen the steepest slide of all. Namely, the fastest and most challenging. In the end it works, but not because of their super powers or exceedingly great wisdom. Instead, because they are on God's path, He is there to pick them up and carry them at His speed, with His safety and protection, all the way to the end. God's rest is not ceasing from action, but getting in on the right action. Find out what God is doing, get involved in His activity, and He will carry you safely to the goal.

So, let's make sure we understand this biblical principle. Rest is not "no more work." Too many Christians think that work is a curse that came from Adam's fall. No, work is reflective of God's creativity and industry. His rest means "no more work in the flesh." In Christ the curse was broken, even the curse on work. You may recall that when Adam and Eve fell into sin way back in the Garden of Eden, the result was that a curse came on their work: "Cursed is the ground for your sake" (Gen. 3:17). Because of this verse and the two that follow, we have long associated work with toil, thorns and thistles, and sweat.

However, before this, humans worked in complete cooperation with God. He did the hard work, and Adam and Eve simply found what He was doing and joined Him in the task. As a result, life in the Garden of Eden was literally heaven on earth. They even enjoyed daily walks with God in the cool of the evening. What a life! What a wonderful existence! And it all came crashing down with the sin of Adam and Eve. For many who have followed, it has never returned. Yet that is a large part of what Christ came to redeem on the cross. The cross is all about salvation, and it is of the highest importance and greatest priority for all. Christ died for our sins and to give us the way (and the only way) to spend eternity with God.

REDEEMING WORK

Another powerful result of Christ's death on the cross was to break the curse off work and redeem that aspect of life to its original status. As I wrote in my second book: "God did not plan for labor to be backbreaking, sweat inducing, anxious toil. Instead, He designed it so humans could help Him care for the earth. Meditate on that for a few moments. Almighty God, for whom nothing is impossible, created the world with a plan for men and women to help tend His creation. Awareness of this reality will revolutionize your attitude toward your Monday-Friday routine."[2]

When Christ died on the cross, in addition to preparing us for eternity, He was enabling us to be ready to live life powerfully and to the full. That is where His rest comes in. When we work in our own strength, we soon begin to realize the results of the curse God pronounced on Adam. Some will fight through it by sheer willpower. You see them every day sweating it out, working an extra shift or a few hours more than the next guy, or struggling with patience and often losing their cool as they scrape and fight to win. The joy has long gone out of the battle. Now it is just mere survival. And some of them seem to be winning. At least their bank account looks like it, but their family life does not.

The rest of God allows you to win all the way around. You have peace at night, your family enjoys you and each other, people are drawn to you, and you still succeed at work. The difference is huge. And it is accomplished through a very simple principle—let go. Did I say simple? It sounds like it, doesn't it? But, as we all know, letting go is not all that easy.

The reason is because we have been programmed differently. We are influenced daily by the dog-eat-dog, beat-the-other-person, work-till-you-drop, get-ahead, grab-for-all-the-gusto world around us. Society emphasizes the necessity of working eighty-hour weeks, pushing and shoving, and getting ahead any way we can. As we observe others, it often seems that the way to the top is paved with smart politicking, flattering the powerful, and stepping on or over anyone who gets in the way. No matter where in the world you live, you know the reality of people who pride themselves on their work ethic. The truth is that often what we call work ethic and what God intended as a work ethic are not the same thing. Indeed, they are miles and worlds apart from each other.

One of my former US clients is a billionaire, who gives millions to Christian causes around the world. His companies employ tens of thousands of workers. He recently told me, "I have never worked more than a forty-hour week." I know of others who toil endlessly while they forsake family and even their health to get ahead, a practice that often costs them the things they love most, and that matter the most. With God it is possible to work smarter, not harder.

I know God wants us to work. I am convinced that He created us to work. And I am not one of those who has never worked more than a forty-hour week. Still, it all comes back to our need to work with God. Let's find what He is doing and watch Him pluck us off the slide and onto His lap as we travel the work slide together.

CHAPTER THREE
SUPERNATURAL REST

"The Lord is my shepherd…He restores my soul"

~ Psalm 23:1 and 3

A friend named Michael is both a gifted minister and business leader. Recently he sold his business, with the terms of the sale including a three-year non-compete agreement. Although that would preclude him from starting another company that would compete with his old one, the provision didn't bother him. Michael had no intention of returning to the business world. He felt sure his future lay in full-time ministry, as a member of a church staff. But all the promises of a position based on his gifts and talents proved to be just empty promises, with no basis in reality. If that weren't bad enough, a while into this fruitless search, he started second-guessing himself. "Maybe this jump from business to church ministry was a bit premature," he thought.

Not only did he miss the excitement of the working world, he realized that business contained all kinds of ministry. After this change of heart, he vowed to renew his job search. Only this time, he wouldn't approach any churches. Although well-qualified, Michael would have to carefully steer clear of his past profession because of the non-compete clause. "No problem," he thought. "I've got a good resume and lots of connections. Surely God will provide." Swallowing his pride, he initiated his new quest for employment. However, as every call turned up nothing and every approach led down a dead end, the pressure began to build. He became moody, unhappy, and irritable. For him, it seemed that his whole life was falling apart. He felt like a beaten man—defeated and discouraged.

However, the most recent time I encountered Michael, his once-troubled countenance had been replaced by an appearance of happiness, peace, and calm. When I asked him how it was going, his response surprised me. "Everything changed suddenly one morning," he said before relating a fascinating story.

He told me about many jobs that looked tailor-made for his experiences and abilities, and yet no one followed up with an invitation to an interview. This included one position a friend described before concluding: "It's perfect for you. They need someone just like you. Apply and the job will be yours." Michael hurried home and filled out an online application. Still nothing. A week later the same friend said: "The job is still open; why didn't you apply?" Michael replied, "I did, but I heard nothing back."

"That's when everything changed," Michael told me. "I realized I was relying on my past success—my good resume, reputation, and hard work to land a position. I realized I hadn't been relying on the Lord."

Yes, during those frustrating weeks he had prayed and continued faithfully serving God. But when it came to his job search, he took all the pressures and possibilities on his own shoulders. The change came when he realized that God already had done the work for him, which meant he could trust the Lord. Michael told me, "That morning I entered into God's rest. I am continuing the search, but I am at peace with where I am, and am fully trusting and resting in the Lord."

This ability to enter into God's rest before the solution comes is the key to finding God's rest in every situation. I can almost hear your thoughts: "That's where I am too, but look what's it's gotten me. Nothing." If that describes your state of mind, then you aren't really there. To discover and fully find the peace of God, it is important that you accept your current life circumstances and all that they bring and say, "Thank you Lord! You have promised to take care of me. In fact, You have promised that You have already done all the work on my behalf. I trust You Lord". It is this ability to step into His rest before you feel anything that gives you the power to fully embrace it.

GOD, THE REST-GIVER

"Come to Me, all you who labor and are heavy laden, and *I will give you rest.* Take My yoke upon you and learn from Me, for I am gentle and lowly in heart, and *you will find rest for your souls.* For My yoke is easy and My burden is light."
(Matt. 11:28-30, emphasis added)

While you may feel as stressed out or as full of doubt as Michael was prior to his realization of God's answer for his troubled spirit, there is a simple formula for entering into God's rest. It is outlined in the passage from Matthew 11. It is so easy that many of us miss it entirely. Notice the seven-step progression in verses 28-30: I will use these steps several times: so let me give you an advance look at the outline.

1. **Come to Me**
2. **Let go of weariness and cares**
3. **Receive the gift of rest**
4. **Let Jesus be your partner**
5. **Learn from the Master**
6. **Practice real humility**
7. **You shall find true peace of mind.**

STEP 1:

COME TO ME

The solution to finding peace of mind, (or entering into God's rest) starts with coming to the Lord and entering His presence. How do we do that? Worship, praise, prayer, and acknowledgement of our lack (of wisdom, strength, or whatever we seek) and His power. We can find rest in studying His Word, communing with Him in prayer, and focusing on Him. As we remove the focus from ourselves, our ability, or others, we can just BE with Him. This may take some time. There are times when I find that place of complete peace and rest after 3 minutes, and on other occasions it may take much longer. While there is no one-size-fits all answer or a simple calendar; you will discover situations where it seems that entering into His presence happens almost immediately. Yet, on other occasions, you may spend minutes or hours in His presence, just soaking there. The answers aren't found in how many minutes, or how many hours, or the amount of effort you exert struggling to be in His presence. That will come from releasing the tight hold you have on your life, and letting God take over.

Come. All you need to do is take a step.
Come. Start singing a praise song.
Come. Simply saying, "Thank you" would be good.
Come. Let go and bask in His presence.

This may sound like "happy talk" or "easy believism," but it isn't. There are some things that only God can do. When you set aside human wisdom, human reasoning, human power, human control, and thirst for worldly riches or power or fame as you seek divine solutions, you will find them.

STEP 2:

LET GO OF WEARINESS AND CARES

There have been times in my life (and I am sure yours as well) that I felt totally exhausted—not from work, but from just thinking about it. You know what I mean: the daily schedule, or even just the thought of it, can wear you out. The Lord wants us to come to Him even before we expend the energy in work. He will pick you up when you are too tired to get up. He offers to lift you up before you even start. By the way, this kind of weariness is not helped by a nap. When you wake up from the nap, you are still tired, and the task still looms over you.

It is so much better to enter into God's rest. Namely, to take advantage of being in His presence in such a way that He carries the load from the beginning. You and I both know that He is not only able to help you, He wants to! Isn't that fantastic? He isn't acting out of a sense of obligation, political connections, influence, or any other of a myriad of human reasons. You're His child and He wants the best for you—even when it doesn't look like it at first.

This passage may be speaking of the need for rest that has come from too much activity, however it appears more likely that the promise is for the kind of rest that we need because of the worries and stress that life can bring to everyone, regardless of income, occupation, social standing, or family connections. This is for one who cannot sleep because of worry and fear. This promise is for those who constantly replay in their mind the worst possible outcome of every situation. This is for the ones who fear failure in every life situation. Or those who face heavy stresses from job, family situations, political dilemmas, or other obstacles, real or imagined.

There is an answer, there is real peace of mind, and it comes in the presence of the Lord!

STEP 3:

RECEIVE THE GIFT OF REST

You see, REST is a gift from God. It is not something that is earned through your own effort. It is not something that is just out of reach or is available to only "the few, the proud, the MARINES." No, rest is a promise from the Father, spoken by Jesus Himself in the context of thanksgiving to the Father for His ways that contradict human intelligence and reasoning. As Christ said in Matthew: "You have hidden these things from the wise and prudent and have revealed them to babes" (Matt. 11:25). Do you see what He is saying? This rest does not come to a special few who have learned the secret. Instead, this rest comes to the masses who will simply—by faith—come to Him.

A passage from Hebrews amplifies this truth: "So I swore in My wrath, 'They shall not enter My rest.' Beware, brethren, lest there be in any of you an evil heart of unbelief in departing from the living God" (Heb. 3:11-12). In other words, the only way to miss this "rest" is unbelief. You must believe in the possibility to receive it. To do this, you must build your faith. An interesting aspect of this rest is its eternal nature. As the following chapter of Hebrews says: "The works were finished from the foundation of the world" (Heb. 4:3). When you cry out to God for help, He does not need to go to work on your behalf. He has already done what needs to be accomplished in order for you to enjoy rest and all that you need!

You receive the gifts of God by faith! This is the essence of a gift . . . believe and receive. The rest is already available. It's been prepared and paid for, and is simply waiting for you to take the step of faith and receive it.

STEP 4:

LET JESUS BE YOUR PARTNER

This is an illustration of how to take on Christ's yoke.

Instead of carrying your own worries, cares, and problems around, try picking up the ones that He is carrying. Meditate on the staggering nature of the sacrifice Jesus made, and what He still bears as our #1 intercessor in heaven. The load is infinitely greater than your worries. Yet He says: "Take my yoke upon you." *The Message* Bible paraphrases the latter part of Matthew 11:28-30 this way: "Walk with Me and work with Me—watch how I do it. Learn the unforced rhythms of grace. I won't lay anything heavy or ill-fitting on you. Keep company with Me and you'll learn how to live freely and lightly."

Most other translations use the word "yoke." So, we need to understand what this means. A yoke consists of a pair of animals joined by a wooden frame, or a support consisting of a frame that allows a person to simultaneously carry two buckets. This means a yoke involves two: Jesus and me. The picture this yields is that I am not carrying this load of job pressures, financial issues, family concerns, or other worldly cares by myself. Instead, I am walking side by side with Jesus. I still have to do my part, but ultimately the outcome is on Christ, not me (or you).

In addition to telling us to take on His yoke, on another occasion Jesus reminded His followers: "I will pray the Father, and He will give you another Helper, that He may abide with you forever" (John 14:16). The way to rest is to understand the truth that you are not walking alone. Jesus is by your side. He is carrying the bulk of the weight; in fact,

He has already carried it to the finish line, and has returned to lift you up and carry it with you to the end.

Remember: it's a faith thing!

STEP 5:

LEARN FROM THE MASTER

You learn the best lessons in life from those who practice what they preach. The best teacher is one who has already walked through what you are facing and struggling with, and can assure you by saying, "This is what I have learned. This is what worked for me." An example is how I tried to write this book several years ago. I knew the principles I wanted to convey, and yet every time I would try to write I would hit "the wall." I believe now, that God needed to first walk me—by experience—through this process. He did not want a theoretical book, but a practical one. That is why this point is so pivotal. Yes, I learned some lessons, and I want to pass them on to you. But while I am the tool the Lord is using today, it is still necessary that you learn from Him.

Jesus said, "Learn from Me." He walked this earth as a man, living life and walking through all the challenges the world could throw at Him. More properly stated, He has always known that, when properly dealt with, life with God by your side is easy. This is why He says, "My yoke is easy."

I will offer more about the specifics of that later.

How do you properly handle this? Look at what Jesus says. Learn from Him.

STEP 6:

PRACTICE REAL HUMILITY

The words that Jesus uses to describe His power, His ability, and His secret weapon might come as a surprise to those used to the braggadocios behavior so often displayed in public life. He says we should be gentle and lowly in heart. Not what we might expect. We have all seen leaders (or even expressed ourselves this way) who are harsh and erratic—demanding, yelling, or cursing to get the response they desire. This is not the Jesus we see in the Matthew 11 passage.

The apostle Paul describes gentle this way: "We were gentle among you, just as a nursing mother cherishes her children" (1 Thess. 2:7). Paul also tells us how to respond to rulers and those in authority: "To obey, to be ready for every good work, to speak evil of no one, to be peaceable, gentle, showing all humility to all men" (Titus 3:1-2).

No matter how radical or counter-cultural it seems, Jesus is telling us the way to rest is by way of a gentle heart. We may think, "God give me rest so that I might become gentle." Instead, Jesus prescribes gentleness so that you can find rest.

STEP 7:

YOU SHALL FIND TRUE PEACE OF MIND

I find it interesting that, in verse 29, Jesus promises: "You will find rest for your souls." This is not a game of hide and seek, as if rest were hidden from us and we had to search relentlessly to uncover it. Instead, it is a process of entering into His presence, giving Him our burdens, and in turn discovering His rest. The kind He describes as rest for your soul.

The Bible teaches us that we are triune beings. As 1 Thessalonians 5:23 puts it, "spirit, soul, and body." "Now may the God of peace Himself sanctify you completely; and may your whole spirit, soul, and body be preserved blameless at the coming of our Lord Jesus Christ." Here Paul is describing how the peace of God can sanctify you completely. When I teach the concept of the triune being in a business context, I tweak the phrase slightly as I change the order to "body, mind, and spirit." The body is where your skills are; the work of your hands. The mind is where your knowledge is; the education you possess. Your spirit is where your values, conscience, purpose, and intuition dwell. It is in the spirit that we connect with the Spirit of God. Realize that this rest is not for your body, but for your mind. Spirit refers to your heart— that part of you that is in communion with the Lord. What Jesus is referring to is a rest that gives you true peace of mind.

Notice that Jesus is not speaking of rest in your spirit, nor of rest for your body. In particular, if He were talking about rest in the physical realm, it would be easy to take a two-hour lunch, go on vacation, or get an extra hour of sleep each night. Instead, He's talking about rest for your soul: your will, your imagination, and your memory. It is rest for that part of you that has a tendency to rethink every situation. It is that part of you that can turn a positive into a negative almost immediately.

I believe what causes our unrest is primarily what happens in the mind. Our sleepless nights stem from a lack of rest in the mind more than any other factor. When our mind is racing out of control, we are wracked by unrest. So, the promise of Jesus has to do with the soul. As I said earlier, this is why taking a nap will not resolve exhaustion, but rest for your soul will.

Jesus closes His promise for rest with this synopsis: "For My yoke is easy and My burden is light." It is easy, because He is carrying the load. It is light, because He has finished the work from the foundation of the world. It is easy, because you cannot gain it through your effort, but through your faith. It is light, because with Christ's yoke, the heaviest portion of weight focuses on Him, not on you. And, it is both light and easy because you can't attain it through hard work, but by the simple process of coming into His presence by faith and receiving.

Come to Me! I will give you rest.

Signed, Jesus

CHAPTER 4
REST FOR PEAK PERFORMANCE

"Jesus said to him, "You shall love the LORD your God with all your heart, with all your soul, and with all your mind." This is the first and great commandment."

~ Matthew 22:37-38

everal years ago, I met a bright young sales executive named Jeff Heilman while speaking at the church he attended in California. Jeff stood out because, as I was speaking, he got out of his seat in the front row, walked up front, and dropped some money on the platform. (He told me later that he felt God grabbing him by the scruff of his neck and dragging him forward). Immediately, I noted Jeff's action and said, "There's someone in here today who could use some money to pay bills, buy groceries, or put gasoline in your car. So, you should come up here and pick it up."

After someone grabbed Jeff's bill, someone else came up and laid more cash on the stage. Someone else came and picked it up, and so on. Over the next twenty minutes, I estimate that more than ten thousand dollars changed hands. As Jeff pointed out, the spirit of poverty can work both ways. People who don't have enough can spend all their time fretting about it, while those who have more than enough are so worried about losing it, they never give any away. In either case, people are being held captive by the spirit of poverty.

Later, Jeff explained the reason for his unusual action that morning was to teach others how to break that spirit of poverty, which God had taught him in the past. To show what that accomplished, despite only attending two years of junior college, he is a mover-and-shaker in the corporate world and has worked with several Fortune 500 companies. That includes handling sales analytics and cloud computing for clients across California. In the past, he directed sales for a start-up company that was later acquired by a major corporation, and worked with one of the nation's leading entrepreneurs.

If the demands of his corporate position weren't enough, Jeff is a happily married man and also the devoted father of seven children. Yet he periodically coaches and mentors others, and volunteers time to two charitable organizations. Recognizing this unusual, spiritually-focused man has a lot to share with the world, I invited him to be a guest on my program, "God@Work," which airs on GodTV, an international television network available online at www.God.tv or in the USA on DirecTV channel 365.

Since I have consulted extensively in the corporate world, I know something about the demands it places on individuals. Add to that the fact that I knew what it was like just to raise two children, let alone seven. That prompted me to ask Jeff the question: "How do you find time to do all of these things?"

His answer surprised me.

"It's energy management more than time management which gives me the angle to do a lot of things," he replied. Then he recalled how the scripture, "With the Lord one day is as a thousand years" (2 Peter 3:8), launched his study of peak performance in athletics and leading business executives. Naturally, Jeff follows sound principles like diet, exercise, and staying well-hydrated. Still, one of his secrets is following consistent cycles of prayer and meditation during the day.

RESTING FOR PERFORMANCE

I found his comments fascinating. As we continued talking, I told him I was writing this book on the rest of God. Jeff mentioned an article from *Harvard Business Review* that had influenced him; later, he sent me a copy. "The Making of a Corporate Athlete" was written by performance psychologists Jim Loehr and Tony Schwartz, who have worked with hundreds of world-class performers in sports, business, medicine, and law enforcement. Acclaimed leadership experts, they also coauthored the book, *The Power of Full Engagement: Managing Energy, Not Time, is the Key to High Performance and Personal Renewal.* It was still selling well more than fifteen years after its release.

In the HBR article, these two sentences particularly caught my eye: "In the living laboratory of sports, we learned that the real enemy of high performance is not stress, which, as paradoxical as it may seem, is actually the stimulus for growth. Rather, the problem is the absence of disciplined recovery." Loehr and Swartz later added this comment: "Chronic stress without recovery depletes energy reserves, leads to burnout and breakdown, and ultimately undermines performance."[1]

They were addressing athletes or corporate executives and how these factors affect their performance. But the same is true for kingdom leaders, business executives, mission's leaders, pastors, and folks like you and me. We have a huge task in front of us. In addition to our responsibilities at work and with our families, we have a divine mandate to reach the world—every nation and every person. To do this, we need to be strong! We cannot allow the stresses of life, in whatever form it may take, to wear us out. We need to learn how to recover. To reinforce Loehr and Swartz's thesis: The problem is the absence of disciplined recovery. Physical rest is the linchpin of recovering from the stress we all face on a daily basis.

PERSONAL RELEVANCE

The idea of rest is of vital importance to me personally. One reason is because I need to know better how to rest amid the serious demands brought on by my leading task—and for all Christians reading this, yours too. That task is doing my part in fulfilling the Great Commission. Nearly every day, I pray about and meditate on how I can be a part of bringing about the fulfillment of the last command of Jesus. By the way, what we refer to as the Great Commission was not named as such by Jesus. One time, the Pharisees were testing Him after He silenced the Sadducees when they tried to trip Him up. So, a Pharisee asked, "Teacher, which is the great commandment in the law?" (Matt. 22:36). That brought this response:

> Jesus said to him, "'You shall love the LORD your God with all your heart, with all your soul, and with all your mind. This is the first and great command-ment. And the second is like it: 'You shall love your neighbor as yourself.' On these two commandments hang all the Law and the Prophets." (Matt. 22:37-40)

So, according to Christ's words, what we call the Great Commission is not even the greatest. But we still refer to it as the Great Commission, a phrase made popular by British missionary Hudson Taylor, the founder of China Inland Mission and a veteran of fifty-one years of service to that nation. Perhaps we call it great in the sense of significance, i.e., in Matthew 28:18-20 Jesus spoke of reaching "all the nations" and "teaching them to observe all things that I have commanded you." Maybe it is because this is the last commandment of Jesus; He delivered these instructions from His full authority. So, we know these were His final instructions before departing from this earth. And, His command is in effect until the "end of the age," as He promised to be with us as we go and make disciples for that duration.

Perhaps it is great in the sense of how it is to permeate all facets of our lives. The command to "go"; or "as you go" and make disciples, suggests that it is something that is to be a part of our everyday lives as individuals, not just part of our church life. Yet, it should be permeating what we do as a church as well.

Because of the biblical instruction recorded from Jesus's time with us, I spend a lot of time dwelling on "how" and "when" and "who" when it comes to the fulfillment of Christ's command. That leads me to often consider its daunting nature. Fulfilling it is obviously too big for one person, one church, one denomination, one missions organization, or even one nation. Yet, at the same time, I must (as we all must) take it personally. So, at that point I start thinking about my preparation for my role. I need to stay sharp, despite reaching my seventies. After all, there is still so much to be done. One of the largest contributors to Christian missions work I know once remarked to me: "I can't retire. There are still souls to be saved."

Thus, the Great Commission mandate is the driving force behind my research on finding and entering the rest of God. Remember, I am not talking about rest in the sense of taking a break, a day off, a vacation, or even going into retirement. I am talking about finding peace of mind in the middle of life's hectic battles and staying strong for the long haul.

FINDING REST

It appears to me that Jesus is addressing the issue of finding lasting rest in Matthew 11:28 when He says, "Come to Me, all you who labor and are heavy laden (stressed out by the world's demands), and I will give you rest." Jesus knew that stress was an issue for everyone on this earth. But He also knew that it was not the real problem. We all face stress and pressures in life, whether it's the corporate CEO answering to an upset board of directors, or a homemaker trying to comfort a flu-ridden child while three others are screaming in her ear. Problems come when we don't deal with stress in an appropriate manner. Christ is the answer.

To return to the *HBR* article that Jeff sent me, it includes this analogy from the world of sports: "In weight lifting, this involves stressing a muscle to the point where its fibers literally start to break down. Given an adequate period of recovery (typically at least 48 hours), the muscle will not only heal, it will grow stronger. But persist in stressing the muscle without rest and the result will be acute and chronic damage."[2]

Can you see the application to your stressed-out life? If you are able to find the rest of God, you will actually gain strength from stress. However, if you stubbornly "push through" without taking time to find any rest or relief, you will reach the point of exhaustion and breakdown. Stress comes in many forms: worry, fear, debt, guilt . . . on and on the list goes. Later, I will review some practical steps for recovery—rest that will result in a stronger army of Great Commission warriors. For now, let's figure out how stress can become a friend instead of our source of unrest.

I once did some consulting with a manager in a high-stress job in a fast-paced, technical environment. She told me how a perplexing situation at her office had caused her considerable turmoil between 2:00 a.m. and 4:00 a.m. the previous night. This wasn't a problem of her own making; she was dealing with it on behalf of someone else. As I talked her through the pattern that Jesus describes in Matthew 11, she began to relax. I talked about making stress her friend and learning from this situation, but not to focus on it so long that it began to harm her. Likewise, remember Christ's gift for you is rest from the stress. You need not be fearful;

remember the wise words Paul wrote to his protégé, Timothy: "For God has not given us a spirit of fear, but of power and of love and of a sound mind" (1 Tim. 5:7). Embrace the power and the sound mind God has given you as you embrace His love. Remember, you are in your job because you love your family. You are doing it for them. So don't let the stress rob you of your joy. Focus on the love aspect of your life and it will help drive out fear.

In this case my counsel worked. It worked because this manager needed it, believed it, and practiced it. It will work for you too, if you will take the steps necessary to see it through. Remember that we are spiritual beings operating in a physical world. In business, most training and education focuses on the physical and mental nature of the work. In other words, your skill set and your knowledge. But, in addition, you need to remember to focus on the spiritual nature of life. Typically, you can't count on your job or career to give you much help in that arena.

SEARCHING FOR SOLUTIONS

Do you see the problem? The very thing that can cause the most turmoil and derailment in your career is stress, which affects you spiritually. However, the answers usually offered have to do with physical and mental conditioning. As a result, we see a work force that is tired, stressed out, and soon becomes incapable of operating at peak performance levels. This can have disastrous consequences physically, emotionally, and mentally.

Stress can provide the motivation to perform more efficiently or quickly in order to meet impending deadlines. However, an overwhelming workload with too many simultaneous demands can contribute to frustration and even panic attacks among those who feel there's not enough time to finish. In their book, *Performance Under Pressure*, authors Heidi Wenek Somaz and Bruce Tulgan say if such conditions routinely lead to overtime or employees having to finish it later at home, the stress of feeling unable to manage their own time can fuel resentment towards the company and negatively impact their commitment and loyalty.

The toll isn't just on the bottom line. Stress means lowered job satisfaction, strained relationships between coworkers, and other problems, according to Bob Losvyk, author of *Get a Grip! Overcoming Stress and Thriving in the Workplace:* "The combined feelings of helplessness and hopelessness generated heightened sensitivities to any and all forms of criticism, defensiveness, and paranoia about job security, jealousy and resentment toward co-workers who seem to have everything under control, short-fuse tempers, diminished self-esteem and withdrawal."[3]

A nationwide survey of thirty-seven thousand Canadian workers between the ages of fifteen and seventy-five found a number of correlations between workplace stress and employee unhappiness and health problems. This was particularly true for shift workers, who routinely face a lack of socializing with family and friends, difficulties planning for personal responsibilities, and struggling to form any semblance of routine in their lives. "It may also be related to the health effects shift work causes," says Jungwee Park, who wrote about the study for that nation's Labour and Household Surveys Analysis Division, "such as disruption of circadian rhythm, reduction in quality and quantity of sleep, fatigue, depression and increased neuoroticism."[4]

For too long, there has been a disconnect when it comes to the incidence of stress and its connection to such physical ailments as headaches, gastrointestinal problems, heart disease, obesity, sleep disorders, and others. Yet we see signs everywhere that the consequences of stress are taking a serious toll on people. Take, for example, the fact that antidepressant use in the US soared 65 percent over a recent fifteen-year period. The Centers for Disease Control says that one in every eight people over the age of twelve uses them, and one-fourth of those surveyed have been taking them for a decade or more.[5]

Such stark statistics make the point that the need to find rest is not just a spiritual issue. It is an eminently practical one too. Now, I have been pointing out that the rest that Jesus is offering is rest for your soul and mind, not your body or spirit. However, it is also true that this very much deals with your spirit—the part of you that connects with God. It is difficult, and probably impossible, to separate your mind from your spirit. So it is with the rest of God; it crosses the gap and deals with both. And without the spiritual connection, you will not find the relief that is necessary to allow you to gain strength from stress.

So, how can we operate at peak performance levels? It is a combination of physical, emotional, mental, and spiritual capacity. When I am called to consult or provide training in the corporate world, I remind the leaders that I am not there to deal with "how to do the work." I tell them I am there to impact the employees at a deeper level, and in most cases how managers deal with others. People skills are what I usually focus on. However, in this book, I am not dealing with how you treat others as much as I am how you treat yourself! In other words, how you can win the victory over the stressful things in your life and career.

In the coming chapters, I will take you through a specific, spiritual adventure toward victory in several of the most common areas of weakness. I will not cover them all, but I will give you a template that will work in every area of your life. How do I know it will work? Because I did not invent it, Jesus did. And Jesus never fails!

CHAPTER 5
A PRACTICAL GUIDE TO REST

*When you make a vow to God, do not delay
to pay it; For He has no pleasure in fools.
Pay what you have vowed —
Better not to vow than to vow and not pay.*

~ Ecclesiastes 5:4-5

Originally, I was going to title this chapter "The Secret to Finding Rest," but then I realized this should not be a secret at all. In fact, there are many times that I have seen others move from a place of complacency and near-boredom to the excitement that stems from following a purpose-driven life. Recently, I watched a man move from the stale, ho-hum position of "comfort" to "excitement." It happened in an almost-overnight fashion. Granted, I have a somewhat vested interest in this story, but without this personal connection, I likely never would have heard it.

This rather lengthy story involves a business executive who—although successful in his career—couldn't envision accomplishing much more in life. He was simply going to carry on until retirement, materially comfortable; but with little sense of purpose or fulfillment. Then he read a book that changed his life. (The connection: it was my first book, *God@Work*. If you want my unbiased opinion of this volume, I'm sorry; I don't have one. My bias is rooted in the fact that I have seen the Lord use it to change many lives. And the truth is, the book still has life changing power today. It is available wherever books are sold.)

This man discovered—yes, discovered, because it is still not widely acknowledged, preached, or practiced—that work and ministry can be the same thing. When he did, it literally changed his life. He could not stop talking about this newly-discovered reality. It changed his demeanor, his countenance . . . even his energy level. It changed his faith and confidence levels as well. He stood taller, walked with a new and more confident stride, and even looked different. God had gifted him with a brilliant business mind. Yet, for some reason he had not connected gifting in business with his desire to serve the Lord.

He had barely cracked open the cover when these comments from the foreword written by evangelist Tommy Tenney jumped out at him: "One of the things that the modern Church has failed to recognize is that just as someone can be anointed to preach or sing, someone can also be *anointed for business.*" The Scripture says that God 'made us kings and priests.' (Rev. 1:6). God ordained the duality of dominions. It's time for man to release what God has recognized!"[1]

Later in the book, I talked about attending a business-ministry summit that included "kings" (businesspersons) and "priests" (pastors) interested in seeing their cities impacted for Christ. There, God confirmed for me what I already knew about the Christian business community: this new breed of ministers was ready to go. They were ready to address the marketplace, the center of society, and to extend their efforts to reach our troubled cities. Spreading the gospel must include their marketplace ministry.

"The individuals who gathered recognized that role, and are beginning to step into it in cities across America and the world," I wrote. "Both the pastors and city-reaching leaders also recognized the role the businessperson has to play in the coming move of God. God is actively working to bring both groups into unity of purpose and function."[2]

That observation grabbed this businessman's attention. So did another in a later chapter: "God is sending out a call to business and professional leaders in the marketplace whom He has strategically trained, mentored, and placed in positions of influence in society, not for their own purposes, but for His."[3]

"Never in my life had I ever heard of someone who had been raised in the modern church—from an infant to an adult—being told that businesspeople were 'anointed for business,'" this business leader told me after we met. "This was jaw-dropping. Indeed, to fail to point this out is what I consider borderline sacrilege by the church leaders and pastors who can be so one-dimensional when it comes to the anointing."

Now, because of a shift in mindset, he was off and running. His future, both in his current position and in others that suddenly opened up to him, looked beautiful and bright. This man is a prime example of "purpose" and "rest" coming together. He did not need to strive for something because he knew that it was God who had given him hope and expectation, mixed with optimism and courage. He not only started making proposals that he would not have made just days before, they were being accepted. Purpose and rest make great companions.

We should be shouting this from the housetops: "There is a clear way to gain the rest that God is promising. And here is the key: knowing your purpose and finding 'rest' go hand in hand." After all, when you know your purpose—the unique reason God put you on earth; that is: why you do what you do—you are on your way to finding total peace of mind.

THE FUEL OF ENERGY

Simply put, when I am working in my purpose, I gain energy as I go through the day. When I am out of my purpose, I can tire easily and want to quit to early. Just as there are things that energize me, there are things that tire me out just thinking about them. Interestingly, my call and purpose include helping you to find your purpose. You will see that later in this chapter, in the "Life Purpose Statement," where I will provide an equation for finding your purpose. It all starts with what the Bible says about purpose. Our purpose in life, as God originally created man, is:

1) To glorify God and enjoy fellowship with Him

The Bible makes it abundantly clear that God created man and that He created him for His glory (see Isaiah 43:7). Therefore, the ultimate purpose of man, according to the Bible, is simply to glorify God.

2) To have good relationships with others

As Jesus said in John 15:12: "This is My commandment, that you love one another as I have loved you."

3) To work

This may come as a surprise to some—especially those who don't like to work. The first commandment that God gave to man had to do with work. Genesis spells this out in two places:

* "Then God said, 'Let Us make man in Our image, according to Our likeness; let them have dominion over the fish of the sea, over the birds of the air, and over the cattle,

over all the earth and over every creeping thing that creeps on the earth'" (Gen. 1:26).

* "Then the LORD God took the man and put him in the Garden of Eden to tend and keep it" (Gen. 2:15).

God gave humankind the mandate to "have dominion" over the creation and to "tend and keep" the garden. In the garden, work was pleasurable because it meant humans acted in cooperation with God. Work brought meaning and fulfillment to life. Work brought joy. Indeed, it was something to look forward to, not an object of dread or feverish attempts to avoid it.

Naturally, everything changed when Adam and Eve fell into sin. Their disobedience affected their relationship with God dramatically, as well as with each other. A curse fell on work; as God told Adam after the fall, "Cursed is the ground for your sake" (Gen. 3:17). The ground was the source of livelihood and the only career available at the dawn of humankind.

When work was cursed, the causes behind "unrest" entered the world. Previously, peace and harmony marked humans' daily existence. Even work was different; when you work in cooperation with God, He does the hard work. As a result, Adam and Eve slept well every night. There were no nightmares, no nagging thoughts, and no worries to keep them awake. No need for sleeping pills or anti-anxiety medications. Even sweat and toil (hard, backbreaking work) came about as a result of sin. So, when someone says to me: "I earned it all by the sweat of my brow," I want to respond with something like: "Congratulations. You have earned it all under the curse."

REDISCOVERING PURPOSE

Only by restoring fellowship with God through faith in Jesus Christ can you rediscover purpose in life. This is exactly what occurred when Jesus died on the cross. As Paul writes: "Christ has redeemed us from the curse of the law, having become a curse for us (for it is written, 'Cursed is everyone who hangs on a tree'), that the blessing of Abraham might come upon the Gentiles in Christ Jesus, that we might receive the promise of the Spirit through faith" (Gal. 3:13-14).

When you receive Jesus Christ as your Savior, you not only receive forgiveness of sin and eternal life in heaven; the curse is broken here on earth. You no longer need to toil in agony, sweating as profusely as a construction worker in the middle of summer, and literally busting a gut to make ends meet. You have a partner, a teacher, and a Redeemer who has broken the curse. He is giving you the promise of "rest."

The reason and purpose behind this book is focused primarily on the third of these calls from God—the call to work. There is no doubt that loving God and loving people are the highest priority; as Jesus told the Pharisee who asked about the greatest commandment: "'You shall love the LORD your God with all your heart, with all your soul, and with all your mind. This is the first and great commandment. And the second is like it: 'You shall love your neighbor as yourself.' On these two commandments hang all the Law and the Prophets" (Matt. 22:37-40).

Yet the call to work as one of God's commands for life often gets overlooked. This is a sad omission, because to find purpose in life—full, meaningful motivation—you must work. Your purpose for existence and your work are closely related. So closely that finding the right fit in your career has a lot to do with your ability to fulfill the call of God on your life. In addition, it certainly adds to the rest that God both promises and wants to give you. With that thought in mind, let's take a closer look at finding purpose.

My equation for finding purpose is:

Passion + Abilities + Your Focus Group = Purpose.

God has made each of us unique. We like different foods, have different interests, and see things differently. As any married couple can tell you, our bodies even respond to heat and cold differently. Yet, when it comes to life purpose, I like to start with passions. I would ask: What are you the most passionate about? Before you answer, let me clarify what I mean by "passion."

A few years ago, I traveled to Afghanistan, where my translator proved to be quite new to the complexities of the

English language. When I spoke of "passion," he only recognized this word in the context of the strong feelings one might have for a person of the opposite sex. No surprise; Dictionary.com lists seven meanings for passion, and the first five have to do with "amorous" feelings. So, I had to work hard to find a word that the translator recognized that could correlate with what I was trying to communicate.

By the way, the last two—non-amorous—meanings given by Dictionary.com are:

- "A strong or extravagant fondness, enthusiasm, or desire for anything: *a passion for music.*
- "The object of such a fondness or desire: *Accuracy became a passion with him.*"[4]

Let me be clear: I do believe that God has created us with a "passion" for a person of the opposite sex. Yet, He clearly has designed those feelings to be acted on only within the context of marriage. From the very beginning, God has given us moral laws governing the subject of sex that are absolute and unchangeable. Nowhere does the Bible teach that sex in itself is a sin. But from Genesis to Revelation, the Bible condemns the wrong use of sex.

Aside from that context, when it comes to finding purpose, passion has to do with enthusiasm and desire. To clarify further, I am going to give a list of things about which we might be passionate, ranging from music to sports to the weather. Yet at this point, my aim is to lead you toward writing your life purpose statement. The first point in my equation is passion. Look at this list and choose from it two or three things that you are passionate about. (Don't worry if your "passion" is not on the list as it is far from exhaustive. I'm just offering it as a starting point for your considerations.)

PASSION

Faith	Family	Health
Friendship	World Peace	Service
Personal Growth	Civil Rights	Children
Literacy	Housing	Culture
Environment	Animals	Art
Sports (fan)	Sports (Active)	Religion
Scholarship	Reading	Education
Destiny	Physical Fitness	Music
Prosperity	Work	

From this list, or a list of your own, write down two or three things that you are really passionate about. For instance, my list would include faith, family, and destiny (purpose).

1. _____

2. _____

3. _____

It is my understanding that these passions come from our Creator. God has made you and me passionate about certain things. In addition, God has given us abilities in these same areas. So, from passion we move to abilities, the second point in my equation. Again, I will give a list—certainly not comprehensive, but a starting point for you to identify your unique abilities. Feel free to add to the list as necessary.

ABILITIES

Write	Create	Manage
Nurse	Nurture	Paint
Counsel	Sing	Build
Draw	Cook	Challenge
Develop	Discern	Pray
Play	Speak	Talk
Organize	Negotiate	Act
Study	Teach	Research
Learn	Lead	Dance
Motivate	Inspire	Solve
Encourage	Plan	Relate

Again, I encourage you to write down two or three of your unique abilities. Mine would include motivate, inspire, and encourage.

1. _____

2. _____

3. _____

Once you have identified your passions and abilities, you are well on your way to finding the divinely-individualized reason or purpose for your life. But we are not done yet. God not only gives us a passion and abilities, He also directs our attentions to certain groups of people. Some are called to Africa as missionaries. Some are called to work with children. Others focus their attention on the disabled, while others work with the elderly. So, let's consider some "people groups" that God has called us to:

FOCUS GROUP

Family	Friend	Customer	Employee
Boss	Stockholder	Vendor	Pastor
Constituent		Neighbor	

OR, GROUPS OF PEOPLE IN:

A nation	A language	An industry	A race
An economic status		A crisis	A city
A neighborhood		Age group	

Or, the leaders in one of seven mountains I referred to in chapter 1:

- Family
- Religion/Faith
- Education
- Government
- Media
- Arts/Entertainment
- Business

In the same way that you identified your passions and abilities, write down two or three people groups that you might feel called to impact.

1. _____

2. _____

3. _____

After I had written down three of my focus groups, I settled on the one I most wanted to reach: business leaders. This ties into the end goal of this whole exercise. Namely, once you have passion, your abilities, and your focus group, you can proceed to write a life purpose statement. Your purpose will likely include or be motivated by your passions, abilities, and focus group. As an example, here is my life purpose statement: "Releasing destiny for business leaders."

This takes my abilities—motivate, inspire, encourage—wrapped into the single word, "releasing"; my passions of faith, family, and destiny distilled in one word: "destiny"; and my focus group, business leaders. From that equation I gave earlier: Passion + Abilities + Your Focus Group = Purpose came my life purpose statement. Therefore, I am in effect fulfilling my life purpose in writing this book!

So, take some time to practice writing a purpose statement. Don't worry (don't leave that place of rest) if you don't get it clear on your first attempt. As you meditate on this task, start using your passion and abilities to reach a focus group. Write it a few times, read it to those who know you best, refine it as you go (and send it to me; I would love to read it: rich@Godisworking.com).

_____

_____

_____

_____

The importance of your purpose as it connects to rest cannot be underestimated. As I meet people around the USA and the world, it has become almost easy to see those who are living lives of purpose. There is a sense of peace and rest that I can see in their face, their mannerisms, their walk, and their conversation. It's not something they can artificially produce. Not something they can manufacture after rehearsing five easy steps. No, it simply exists as part of their being.

Remember the friend I told you about at the beginning of this chapter? You can see "purpose" on his face and discern the "rest" in his countenance. The same should be your goal as you seek to find God's destiny for the unique you that He has blessed the world with. Remember: find purpose, find rest. It's the best life plan out there.

CHAPTER 6

FACING THE DEBT MONSTER

*For the love of money is a root of all kinds of evil,
for which some have strayed from the faith in their
greediness, and pierced themselves through with
many sorrows.*

~ 1 Timothy 6:10

We have been through the basics—what the Bible says about rest, illustrations of how you can attain rest, and some of God's promises. technically, you have what you need to know to enter into God's rest. However—because I've dealt with thousands of people in corporate and ministerial settings—I know that you likely still need some form of encouragement. Since we aren't together right now, I can't verbally tell you some next steps, issue a personal challenge, or deliver some additional motivation. However, I'm going to give you a strategy for avoiding some of the biggest mindsets that keep you from entering into God's rest.

There are many issues that can cause stress (another way of saying, "lack of rest" of "lack of peace of mind."); you will find that one feeds off another. I talked about physical stress earlier when talking about the corporate athlete. Now I am talking about stress that affects your mind. With this kind of stress one stressor can lead to another. For example, debt will bring the added stressors of worry, guilt, and shame. In much the same way, guilt will bring shame and worry. If your issue is lust (a mind-controlling obsession or compulsion), that will bring shame and guilt. Continuing this analysis, we can see that fear will bring worry, and anger will connect with fear and shame.

For these strategies I am going to again rely on the outline from Christ's teaching in Matthew 11:28-30. Stick with me; I know you have already read about it in chapter 3 and think you don't need any more from that passage. Wrong! We all need a lot more. Remember, this is Jesus speaking. He is the ultimate giver of all things. I am simply a tool to lead you to a place where you can find peace of mind. Learn from Jesus!

In this chapter I will address the enemy of debt. With credit card debt reaching an all-time high lately, this is a biggie for sure. Before you space me out by saying, "I don't need this one, I have no debt" . . . before you close the book and move on . . . insert "money" in place of debt. You see, many wealthy people obsess over money. Even if they're not in debt, they worry about things like:

- I don't have enough.
- I can't pay my bills.
- What about my retirement?
- What if the economy crashes (and in your mind you add: I'm sure it will)?

On and on we could go. Still didn't hit your "money problem" button? Then insert your own preoccupation, whether big or small. If it is controlling your mind and robbing you of the peace and rest that God wants to give you, then you need to deal with it. Don't count this chapter out just because I don't know you that intimately. Remember, we are learning from Jesus and He knows.

The debt monster originates with a familiar stronghold: money. A primary reason the Bible teaches us to give to God's work is because God knows how hard it is for us to let go of our money. When we give generously, it is a statement affirming our faith in God, a sign of our assurance that He will bring us ways to replace it. Or, miraculously replace it Himself.

To illustrate this point, I need to share a story about a man who is now a good friend. He came to the church I then pastored not because he was a Christian, but to satisfy his wife. Most people in their circle of friends also attended, so he ended up there even though he had no idea what "church" was supposed to look like.

I learned a lot from this man, especially since he saw things differently than those who were raised in church. He taught me to refine my messages when he commented: "You talked through your sale today, pastor. I was ready to say 'yes' and you just kept on talking." After several years of attending services, he made a decision to follow Christ.

He then taught me about freedom from debt. I knew some biblical principles about debt, but he showed me its meaning in real life terms. One Sunday, he asked if he could give a testimony before the offering. Although a bit concerned—not for what he might say, but how this rough-talking guy might say it—I agreed. His testimony went something like this:

"As you all know, I have been sitting in these services for a long time. A few weeks ago, when the pastor started talking about tithing, it upset me so much that I whispered to my wife loud enough that the whole row heard me say, 'I am tired of all this talk about money and tithing; if he does it one more time I'm going to get up and leave.' Well, my friend down the row heard me and replied, 'Don't knock it 'til you have tried it.' That made sense, so I tried it. We were deep in debt at that time—thousands of dollars in debt. But I started tithing, and guess what? It works. All of our debt is gone. I don't know how. I just know that God did it. And so, folks, if you are not tithing, you are just plain stupid."

That was it. One of the most powerful testimonies on tithing I have ever heard.

Now, I will not call you stupid, but I will say this: God's principles really do work. What Jesus is teaching in Matthew 11 is real life stuff. So, if you're ready, let's look at the seven steps to find peace of mind.

STEP 1:
COME TO ME

Jesus said: "COME TO ME!" Get into God's Presence!

To offer some context for Matthew 11:28-30, in this passage Jesus is thanking the Father for revealing truths that had been hidden from the wise and the prudent. In verse 25, Jesus even refers to those who can receive these truths as babes. Don't think yourself as too wise, too experienced, or that you know it all. Remember, you would be matching wits with the Son of God. That is a mind battle that you cannot ever hope to win. Jesus goes on to say, "Even so, Father, for so it seemed good in your sight. All things have been delivered to Me by My Father" (Matt 11:26-27). It is okay to be like a babe in the presence of Jesus. To be with Him is to be with the Father!

First, let's deal with the elephant in the room. My purpose here is not to deal with either the poverty teaching that some declare to be from God, or the "name it and claim it" teaching that others declare to be from God. I have strong— and, I believe, biblically-based convictions—on the subject of money, prosperity, and wealth, but that teaching would distract from my point. I am talking about those whose mental lives are torn apart by debt. They are injured so badly they can't sleep, can't focus, and can't concentrate on much of anything. Debt with a capital D is consuming their life.

Or, on the other end of the spectrum, there are those who have plenty of money and yet fret constantly that they don't have enough, or that they will lose it, or the economy will crash and wipe it out. After all, that has happened during several stock market crashes over the past century. Over the years, in meeting and dealing with a number of individuals, I have discovered that people with lots of money can stress over it more than those who have very little.

So, no matter how big this debt problem is, and no matter how much you obsess over money, let's not start with the problem. Let's start with the answer: "Come to Me!" So, how do you do that? Entering into God's presence may come in silence, such as in meditation and prayer. Or, it may come in loud, high-decibel praise music in a worship service. Or, in your car or at home in your quiet place. (Sometimes the "quiet place" gets really loud with God's voice.) But, for sure, entering God's presence comes by deliberate focus.

Let's try a quiet one. Read Psalm 91 out loud. (I know I said quiet, but I did not mean silent.) There is power in your words, and the Word becomes more powerful when you read it, declare it, proclaim it out loud. Let's go:

"He who dwells in the secret place of the Most High shall abide under the shadow of the Almighty."

You might want to stop here for a moment and give thanks to God: "Thank you Lord, that there is a secret place, and I am going to dwell there in your presence. I am abiding with you. Nothing shall harm me when I am in this place."

"I will say of the LORD, "He is my refuge and my fortress; my God, in Him I will trust."

Oh Lord, I trust you. Help me to trust you more!

**"Surely He shall deliver you from the snare of the fowler and from the perilous pestilence.
He shall cover you with His feathers,
and under His wings you shall take refuge;
His truth shall be your shield and buckler.
You shall not be afraid of the terror by night . . . "**

Maybe you wake up in the middle of the night . . . or you can't even get to sleep because your mind won't stop telling you that your debt will be your ultimate destruction. Here is God's promise: deliverance. You need not face peril, because He is your covering, your refuge, and your shield. With God, fear is gone. Declare it now: "Fear, you have no place in my life. I am accepting as truth the Word of the living God and I am living in His rest."

**"Nor of the arrow that flies by day,
Nor of the pestilence that walks in darkness,
Nor of the destruction that lays waste at noonday."**

If you can win this battle in the night, the day will be much easier. But God has an answer for the daylight battles as well.

"A thousand may fall at your side,
And ten thousand at your right hand;
But it shall not come near you.
Only with your eyes shall you look,
And see the reward of the wicked.

Because you have made the LORD, who is my refuge,
Even the Most High, your dwelling place . . . "

You see, coming to His presence is not for an occasional visit—your goal is to live in His presence! You need a mindset change here. You must declare, "I will not come and go with regard to being in the presence of the Lord! I will dwell with Him night and day, at home and at work. At rest, while I sleep, and in activity while I exercise."

"No evil shall befall you,
Nor shall any plague come near your dwelling;

For He shall give His angels charge over you,
To keep you in all your ways.
In their hands they shall bear you up,
Lest you dash your foot against a stone."

You feel like you're fighting a big enemy? Remember, God has given His angels charge over you. You think the demons of hell are something? Not compared to God's angels. Besides, God has two angels to each of the devil's demons.

"You shall tread upon the lion and the cobra,

The young lion and the serpent you shall trample underfoot."

Don't try it, just believe it.

"Because he has set his love upon Me, therefore I will deliver him;
I will set him on high, because he has known My name.
He shall call upon Me, and I will answer him;
I will be with him in trouble;
I will deliver him and honor him.
With long life I will satisfy him,
And show him My salvation."

It is time for the quiet place to become the place of praise! Lift a shout to the Lord, wherever you are—unless perhaps, you are on an airplane or in your cubicle at work. In that case, a quiet, but audible, "Praise the Lord" will do. Among other ways to get into God's presence are quietly meditating on His Word or in prayer, singing, or prayer walking.

STEP 2:

Let Go of Weariness and Cares

Jesus said: "COME

Jesus calls on all "who labor and are heavy laden."

Matthew 11:28

I recommend that you get really practical with your debt or other money issue by writing it down. Get it out in the open. List the total amount of what you owe and the monthly obligations to service that debt. Include a few ideas about ways you can address it. The point to this exercise is to help you get a tangible picture of it. Not only can you see it, you can lay it at Jesus feet and picture it gone. At this point, this is a faith issue. The question is: Do you really believe the word of God, or are you trusting in the flesh—or, even more damaging—believing the lies of the enemy?

Here are some practical steps.

1. Did this money problem result from mistakes, failures, or sin on your part? If so, then simply repent. After all, the God we serve is a forgiving God who promises: "If we confess our sins, He is faithful and just to forgive us our sins and to cleanse us from all unrighteousness" (1 John 1:9).

2. Did this debt come because you failed to believe God; was there a lack of faith on your part? Those of you who are stressed out about the direction of the stock market or what will happen next year with the economy, or other fears (real or imagined) need to refocus your faith on the Lord. To help build your faith, read out loud some of His promises:

   • "And you shall remember the LORD your God, for

it is He who gives you power to get wealth, that He may establish His covenant which He swore to your fathers, as it is this day" (Deut. 8:18).

- "Now if God so clothes the grass of the field, which today is, and tomorrow is thrown into the oven, will He not much more clothe you, O you of little faith? Therefore do not worry, saying, 'What shall we eat?' or 'What shall we drink?' or 'What shall we wear?' For after all these things the Gentiles seek. For your heavenly Father knows that you need all these things. But seek first the kingdom of God and His righteousness, and all these things shall be added to you" (Matt. 6:30-33).

- "Beloved, I pray that you may prosper in all things and be in health, just as your soul prospers" (3 John 2).

3. Consider the power of your words. Wise King Solomon wrote, "Death and life are in the power of the tongue, and those who love it will eat its fruit" (Prov. 18:21). When you are speaking negative words over your finances, or over your life in general, you are holding yourself hostage to those words. But realize this: according to Proverbs 18:21, the same power in your words that can put you in bondage can also set you free. When you speak the powerful words of scripture and faith over your life: something happens on your behalf.

To recap, if you are enslaved to money—be it debt or an unhealthy obsession with it—it likely comes from your own mistakes (sin or bad judgment), lack of faith, or using foolish worry in place of good, prayer-initiated faith. So, repentance and faith building is necessary. This can only come from extended time spent with the Lord. So determine a time (no better way to start the day than in prayer) you can meet with God and spend that time with Him. He will give you rest.

STEP 3:

RECEIVE THE GIFT OF REST

When Jesus said, "I will give you rest" that was/is a promise that He is fully able to fulfill. Many Christians have been so programed by a religion of works that emphasizes performance over grace that they have a hard time receiving a gift of grace. We have been told, "You must do this" or "You must do that." While not necessarily in these exact words, many of us have been told, "God is not happy with you and so you need to (whatever the misled parent, teacher, or pastor deemed necessary)." By the way, I have been all three of those—maybe not to you, but to others. And so, right now consider me as that person of influence in your life so we can deal with it. Okay? I will say to you: "I am sorry for how I hurt you, misled you, or improperly influenced you. I did not mean to hurt you, but I did! Please forgive me."

If you practice this and are sincere I know it will feel good. I know it feels good because I have done it many times. Dealing with past hurt through forgiveness is a powerful tool to gain the rest of God and true peace of mind. Forgiveness is the #1 gift Jesus offers. Indeed, Jesus loves you so much that He died for you! Surely He is able to keep this promise: "I will give you rest." Receive it by faith!

STEP 4:

LET JESUS BE YOUR PARTNER

Do you remember the day you accepted Christ as your Savior? You invited Jesus into your heart and to take over your life. And He came in. He is with you, living in you, and abiding with you every day. Everywhere you go, He is there. By the way, if you have not invited Him in, do that right now. His only requirement is faith! If you can believe in Him, He will enter into your life right now.

The phrase Jesus uses in verse 29 is "take my yoke." As I mentioned earlier, that speaks of two that are connected together. The difference is that He is carrying much more of the load. I heard a colorful tale about this truth several years ago while traveling in Africa. A pastor dressed in a long, flowing, multi-colored robe shared with us what he called "an African parable." (It is short, so listen fast.)

"The elephant and the mouse crossed the bridge together. And when they got to the other side, the mouse said: 'Didn't we make that bridge shake?"

That, my friend, is what this step is all about. In the parable, we are the mouse; Jesus is making it all happen. But we get to share in it. Partner with Jesus and win the victory over debt! "Didn't we make that bridge shake?"

STEP 5:

LEARN FROM THE MASTER

Later in verse 29, Jesus says to "learn from Me." Watch Me. Listen to Me. Imitate Me. Imagine this—Jesus is offering to be your teacher! We have seen it over and over again in life. A great teacher makes a huge difference in a students' learning ability. A good coach can take a poor or mediocre team and in a short time turn them into champions.

Let me illustrate from a very American mindset. I am a football fan, especially of the University of Nebraska Cornhuskers. Not that many years ago, their football team was one of the best in the nation; historically, they have won more than 70 percent of their games. However, in recent years the team has weakened. They sandwiched a 9-4 record in 2016 around marks of 6-7 and 4-8.

After the bleak 2017 season, the school decided it was time for a new coach. So, they hired Scott Frost, the last quarterback to lead the Huskers to a national championship. However, it is not his record as a player several years ago that had hopes soaring headed into the 2018 season. It was his record as a coach. Two years earlier, Frost became the head coach for a team that had not won a single game the year before he came. His first year as head coach, the University of Central Florida won six games and lost six games. The next year, he led UCF to its first-ever undefeated season, including thumping seventh-ranked Auburn in the Peach Bowl. Now, Frost was coming home to coach the Huskers. Across Nebraska, there were a lot of fans with great faith proclaiming, "The new coach will lead us back to national prominence."

Did I believe it? Sure, I'm a faithful fan.

But I will tell you what I believe a lot more. Jesus is the greatest teacher, coach, mentor, example and Savior that has or ever will exist.

LEARN FROM HIM!

STEP 6:

PRACTICE REAL HUMILITY

Jesus describes Himself as "gentle and lowly in heart." The New Living Translation translates the middle part of verse 29 as: "Because I am humble and gentle at heart."

Now remember, Jesus just advised us to "learn from Me." What are we to learn from the Son of the Living God, the Redeemer of the world, the only sinless One to ever live? Humility. If there was ever one who could claim it all . . . "I know it all because I created it all; I know it all because My Father and I hold it all together" . . . it is Jesus. As Paul writes of Him: "He is the visible image of the invisible God. He is supreme over all creation, because in connection with him were created all things—in heaven and on earth, visible and invisible, whether thrones, lordships, rulers or authorities—they have all been created through him and for him. He existed before all things, and he holds everything together" (Colossians 1:15-17 CJB).

Yet, with that kind of resume, He says, "I am humble and gentle." In light of that, I would ask: What do I have to brag about? And if you need more insight here; then consider this: "Therefore He says: 'God resists the proud, but gives grace to the humble'" (James 4:6).

The question is this: Do you want the hand of God held out to you like a stop sign? Or do you want the hand of God calling to you, motioning to you to come to Him? Your rest in God will come when you lay your pride down and walk in humility before the Lord.

STEP 7:

FIND TRUE PEACE OF MIND

I offer this prayer for you. Pray it out loud; silent prayer or praying in your head is for another time. Now . . . speak it out. I know that we have already prayed through Psalm 91, but now let's add this scripture-filled prayer.

Father, forgive me for the sin of not fully trusting You with my finances! I know that I cannot handle this alone. I need your help daily, even hour by hour. And so right now I turn to Your Word and declare: I will be anxious for nothing, but in everything by prayer and supplication, with thanksgiving, I will make my requests known unto You (Phil. 4:6). I know that "God shall supply all your need according to His riches in glory by Christ Jesus" (Phil. 4:19). So today I choose to follow Psalm 37:4-5: "Delight yourself also in the LORD, and He shall give you the desires of your heart. Commit your way to the LORD, trust also in Him, and He shall bring it to pass."

Today, I make this declaration: I am debt free. I am fully trusting in You and therefore I shall not fear. I shall not walk in doubt. You said: "Ask, and it will be given to you; seek, and you will find; knock, and it will be opened to you. For everyone who asks receives, and he who seeks finds, and to him who knocks it will be opened" (Matt. 7:7-8). I am living in the presence of the One who said, "Come to me and I will give you rest" and I receive that promise right now. This prayer I pray in the powerful name of Jesus, fully trusting in His Word.

Can I get an "amen"?

CHAPTER 7

FINDING REST IN TIMES OF FEAR

"Perfect love casts out fear."

~ 1 John 4:18

A leader in a church I once pastored battled fear for many years. This woman's problem began with a medication her doctor prescribed following surgery. It caused such a traumatic reaction that she felt sure she was about to die. Fear came and stayed with her for years. Often, she would awaken her husband with the plea: "Pray for me; I think I'm dying."

Ironically, despite relatively good health, she battled this unrealistic fear of dying for several years. There were times it was so debilitating she would not go out in public for weeks, or even months. The fear persisted until one night when, she recalled, "The Lord woke me up and told me, 'The answer to your fear is at your fingertips.'"

She looked over and noticed her Bible on the bedside stand. Following the Lord's step-by-step instructions, she went out to the family room and began to read. As she read the Word of God out loud, He healed her fear completely. In fact, not only did God remove this ongoing issue with fear, she experienced physical healing of some other, unrelated issues that she had been dealing with for years. Her testimony is powerful evidence of the success you can have by following the template in this chapter. You need soul rest far more than you need physical rest: release from tension, worry, stress, and guilt. And, release from fear, bitterness, and anxiety. Release brings soul rest. This is the key to real peace.

Stay with me. I am writing with the goal of releasing you from bondage and bringing you to a place of rest. In the previous chapter, I covered a strategy for rest when debt or money issues have you worried, stressed out, or unable to focus or sleep. Using Christ's same template from Matthew 11:28-30, but with totally different applications, I will now tackle several others. You may find one or more of these a bigger battle for you, which means you may need to focus more efforts there. But I believe that at one time or another, most of us will face all of these enemies of rest.

Here is a brief outline of what we will cover in the next several chapters:

✔ Fear: To again quote the verse that opens this chapter, "Perfect love casts out fear" (1 John 4:18).

✔ Worry: Why worry when you can pray? (See the chorus that opens chapter 8).

✔ Anger: "Do not let the sun go down on your wrath" (Eph. 4:26).

✔ Guilt: As I like to say, guilt is from the devil, but conviction is from the Lord.

✔ Shame: "When pride comes, then comes shame; but with the humble is wisdom" (Prov. 11:2).

✔ Lust: "Walk in the Spirit, and you shall not fulfill the lust of the flesh" (Gal. 5:16).

PERFECT LOVE CASTS OUT FEAR

Whatever the crisis, when fear looms large in your life, it is time to bring your faith to bear. Follow these seven steps:

STEP 1:

COME TO ME

Coming into God's presence is an interesting phrase; it seemingly assumes that we are not abiding in His presence. Yet, as we all know, we can abide in Him all the time. When

I received Jesus as my Lord and Savior, He came into my life and now He lives in me. So, let me define this phrase a little more specifically. When I refer to the words of Jesus and His statement, "Come to Me," I believe that He intended for this to be a conscious, deliberate act of entering into His presence. Think about this. Jesus does not just live in me, as in: "He has taken up residence in my life." It is more than that. He has taken ownership in my life. My life is not my own; it belongs to Him.

So when I "come to Him" this is not as much an action of moving toward Him as it is a statement of faith and acknowledgement that He is the owner, controller, and Savior of my life. With that thought in mind, bring your fear into His presence and let this scripture break that bondage:

> "The LORD is my light and my salvation;
> *Whom shall I fear?*
> The LORD is the strength of my life;
> *Of whom shall I be afraid?*
> When the wicked came against me
> To eat up my flesh,
> My enemies and foes,
> They stumbled and fell." (Ps. 27:1-2, emphasis added)

STEP 2:

LET GO OF WEARINESS AND CARES

Here, we must become both very honest and very open. What is it that is causing fear? Though quite familiar to many from a church background, this acronym on fear has always been quite helpful for me. Fear is:

F — false
E — evidence
A — appearing
R — real

Granted, there are times when the fear is real. We may be facing foreclosure on our mortgage, a catastrophic illness, rebellious children, an imminent corporate downsizing, or serious addiction issues, either personally or with a loved one. But no matter what the situation, when we allow the light of God's Word to shine on it and allow God's power to be manifested against it, we find it to be exactly what the acronym suggests—false evidence appearing real.

This is true even when you think that fear is the rational response. It may well be a most daunting and fear-inducing crisis. The bank has already sent you an eviction notice, you have a child whose court hearing is next week, or the doctor has delivered a foreboding diagnosis with the serious conclusion: "There's nothing more we can do." On those occasions, we must still deal with this fear in a faith-filled way. So, get it out in the open. Speak the Word, not just the word of fear. You must learn to speak the word of faith. This kind of fear will rob you of sleep, so prepare your mind before sleep with the Word of the Lord that can bring victory.

Once again, here are some practical steps.

- Did this fear come to you as a result of mistakes, failures or sin on your part? If so, then repent. The same verse I mentioned in chapter 6 regarding money applies here: "If we confess our sins, He is faithful and just to forgive us our sins and to cleanse us from all unrighteousness" (1 John 1:9).

- Did this fear come because you failed to believe God? In other words, was there a lack of faith on your part? In every circumstance, we must face the facts from a practical standpoint before we recall the promises of God. Remember, His report is the report that we must believe. Faith must rise up to bring us into a place of peace and rest. Consider these promises from God:

"Bless the LORD, O my soul;
And all that is within me, bless His holy name!
Bless the LORD, O my soul,
And forget not all His benefits:
Who forgives all your iniquities,
Who heals all your diseases,
Who redeems your life from destruction,
Who crowns you with lovingkindness and tender mercies,
Who satisfies your mouth with good things,

So that your youth is renewed like the eagle's."
(Ps. 103:1-5)

From this passage of Scripture, my wife, Wilma, and I pray this brief prayer nearly every day: "I thank you Lord, that I am saved, healed, delivered, protected, preserved, and made whole." The reason we can make such a statement is we are:

- Saved because God "forgives all your iniquities" (v. 3)
- Healed because He "heals all your diseases" (v. 3)
- Delivered because the Lord "redeems your life from destruction" (v. 4)
- Protected because He "crowns you with lovingkindness and tender mercies" (v. 4)
- Preserved because God "satisfies your mouth with good things" (v. 5)
- Finally, we are made whole "so that your youth is renewed like the eagle's" (v. 5)

Consider the power of your words—the truism from Proverbs 18:21 that I pointed out in chapter 6. Namely, that both death and life emanate from your tongue. So when you speak out the truths from Psalm 103:1-5, these scriptures offer healing and deliverance from your fear. Here are a couple that you should speak out loud every day until the fear is gone (do not skip this step; read and declare these scriptures out loud—with faith!)

"I sought the LORD, and He heard me,
And delivered me from all my fears." (Ps. 34:4).

If you walk in My statutes and keep My commandments, and perform them, then I will give you rain in its
season, the land shall yield its produce, and the trees of
the field shall yield their fruit. Your threshing shall last
till the time of vintage, and the vintage shall last till the
time of sowing; you shall eat your bread to the full, and
dwell in your land safely. I will give peace in the land,
and you shall lie down, and none will make you afraid;
I will rid the land of evil beasts, and the sword will not
go through your land. You will chase your enemies, and
they shall fall by the sword before you. Five of you shall
chase a hundred, and a hundred of you shall put ten
thousand to flight; your enemies shall fall by the sword
before you. (Lev. 26:3-8)

Let me recap. If you are enslaved by FEAR, either real or
imagined, it may come from either your own mistakes (sin
or bad judgment) or lack of faith—or foolishness in place of
good, prayer-initiated faith. So, repentance and faith building
are necessary, which can only come from spending extended
time with God. So, just as I said in step 2 in dealing with worries about money, determine a time—likely in the morning—
you can spend time with Him. He will give you rest.

STEP 3:

RECEIVE THE GIFT OF REST *(In spite of your fear!)*

This truth goes against the grain of rugged American independent, self-reliant, tough-guy-earn-your-own-way-and-pull-yourself-up-by your-bootstraps kind of thinking: The rest of God is only available as a gift. You cannot earn it, you cannot buy it, and you cannot work hard enough or study long enough to deserve it. It is a gift. Jesus said: "I will give you rest." Fear will tell you that you don't deserve it. Even if that were true . . . so what? Jesus did not say, "Make yourself worthy and I will give you rest." He said, "Come to Me . . . and I will give you rest." It is a gift. Gifts are not meant to be wrapped in pretty paper and then placed out of sight on a shelf. They are meant to be received. It is always good to say, "Thank you." So thank the Lord for His gift, His gift of peace, and let Him resolve your issue with fear.

STEP 4:

LET JESUS BE YOUR PARTNER

A yoke is a symbol of partnership. There are two of you working on it, not just one. Jesus says, "I will help you out with your problems. I will help carry your load." He doesn't add to your load. He shares it. After all, He doesn't have a load. He's God! He says, "I will share your load. Stick with

Me. Go shoulder to shoulder with Me. Work with Me and I will be your partner; I will carry a part of your load." And when He says, "I will carry part of your load," what He means is He will take the heavy part and leave you with the easy part. So, when He says, "My yoke is easy and My burden is light," it is because we're sharing the load and He's shouldering the heavy part.

This whole passage is about learning and working. Think about this: Jesus invites us to take His yoke—a work implement. Jesus is not proclaiming that we need a vacation or that it's time to retire. He is talking about work, and how He wants to help us with it. So, when fear arises in a work context, get in the yoke with Jesus. There is no fear here. He can handle your pay scale; He can arrange a raise much easier than you can lobby for one. I was talking with a woman recently who works for a large company, where executives in another division offered her a promotion to come to work in their division. Although that came with a big raise, she prayed and did not feel the Lord's peace about it, so she refused. The next week her boss—who knew nothing about the offer—told her they were giving her a raise. An even bigger raise than the new job would have meant.

Get in the yoke with Jesus. He can handle your fear!

STEP 5:

LEARN FROM THE MASTER

It is lesson time, so learn from Jesus. Did He ever face fear? Had we been in His place—facing hatred, scorn, humiliation, and death when His only "crime" was upsetting the political and religious elites of His day—You or I would have felt fear. But Jesus is our example, and He says, "Learn from Me."

Was there fear for Jesus? This I know: He faced the cross alone. Even God had turned His back when Jesus was facing the moment when He won the victory for you and me. He said seven things from the cross. Six were full of hope, even of victory. Let's look at these verses from the New Testament:

Father, forgive them, for they know not what they do. (Luke 23:34)

Today you will be with Me in paradise. (Luke 23:43)

He said to His mother, "Woman, behold your son!" Then He said to the disciple, "Behold your mother!" (John 19:26-27)

I thirst! (John 19:28)

It is finished. (John 19:30)

Father, into your hands I commit my spirit. (Luke 23:46).

However, the seventh echoes a depth of despair I cannot fathom:

"My God, my God, why have you forsaken me?" (Matt. 27:46).

But this much I know: He did it for me. Therefore, I need

not fear even death. Because at the lonely moment on the cross, victory was assured. Here is the lesson. You need not fear being abandoned by your loving Father, because even that travesty was handled by Jesus.

STEP 6:

PRACTICE REAL HUMILITY

The reason to practice humility can be found at the beginning of Psalm 34:

I will bless the LORD at all times;
His praise shall continually be in my mouth.
My soul shall make its boast in the LORD;
The humble shall hear of it and be glad.
Oh, magnify the LORD with me,
And let us exalt His name together.

I sought the LORD, and He heard me,
And delivered me from all my fears. (Ps. 34:1-4)

Notice how deliverance from fear is connected to blessing, praise, exalting the name of the Lord; and humility. "The humble shall hear of it and be glad . . . and (He) delivered me from all my fears." When you approach your fears in your own strength, you have no reason for pride or boasting. When you realize that only Jesus can relieve your fears and give you rest in the middle of the storm, you arrive at the state of humility.

STEP 7:

YOU SHALL FIND TRUE PEACE OF MIND

Go to the Lord. Here's a suggested prayer for facing fear:

I come before you today, Lord, knowing that I live in a place of fear and opposition to You and the power of Your Word. I want to approach Your throne in faith instead of this nagging fear that grips my heart and soul. I do not want to be focused on the anxieties of everyday living. Starting today, my motto will be: To fear nothing and pray about everything.

For too long, I have allowed the enemy of my soul to keep me focused on negative thought patterns. Now, by Your Spirit, I ask You to lead me out of this pit. Take me away from this dark place and into the authority of Your Word. These everyday fears are minor ones, but they are still fears and they still hinder the lifestyle I desire—one of prayer and praise—by keeping me focused on fear and anxiety. I desire to live in Your place of rest. I want to say as Paul did: For (I) did not receive the spirit of slavery to fall back into fear, but (I) have received the Spirit of adoption as sons, by whom (I) cry, "Abba! Father!" (Rom. 8:15).

You are putting a new song in my mouth, a hymn of praise to You. I will declare as the Psalmist did: "Blessed is that man who makes the LORD his trust, and does not respect the proud, nor such as turn aside to lies (Ps. 40:4). . . . Whenever I am afraid, I will trust in You (Ps. 56:3). . . . I will say of the LORD, 'He is my refuge and my fortress; my God, in Him I will trust'" (Ps. 91:2).

I will trust in you, Lord, with all my heart. I will do what Proverbs 3:5-6 teaches; I will lean not on my own understanding. I will acknowledge God in everything so He will direct my paths. My cry will be as the prophet Isaiah's: "Behold, God is my salvation, I will trust and not be afraid; 'for YAH, the LORD, is my strength and song; He also has become my salvation" (Isa. 12:2). I will pay attention to the words of Moses as he prepared to lead Israel into the Promised Land: "The LORD himself goes before you and will be with you; he will never leave you nor forsake you. Do not be afraid; do not be discouraged" (Deut. 31:8 NIV). I will remember the Psalm: "The LORD is on my side; I will not fear. What can man do to me?" (Ps. 118:6).

Father, because of Your Word, I have received the spirit of wisdom and revelation in the knowledge of God. So, I make a covenant with You today to always give voice to Your Word. I will no longer give voice to the enemy. I will give no place to the devil. Instead, I give place to the Spirit of God. You have given angels charge over me in all ways and my way is the way of the Word. Your Word will cause me to prevail over the darkness. My pathway is freedom from fear and anxiety. Amen and Amen! I will rest in You!

CHAPTER 8
WHY WORRY WHEN YOU CAN PRAY?

*"Therefore I say to you, do not worry
about your life...."*

~ Matthew 6:25

Why worry when you can pray?
Trust Jesus He'll be your stay
Don't be a doubting Thomas
Rest fully on His promise
Why worry worry worry worry
When you can pray?[1]

As a youngster, the first time I ever heard of worry was when we sang this little chorus in Sunday school. It was written by John W. Peterson in 1949 (and yes, I was a five-year-old in 1949). Peterson wrote and published over one thousand songs. His career as a singer and songwriter was interrupted by a stint as a pilot in World War II, when he flew over what was known as the China Hump. During the war, Allied pilots bestowed that name on the eastern end of the Himalayan Mountains. They flew military transport planes over the Hump on flights from India to China, in order to supply Chinese forces led by Chiang Kai-shek and US Air Force troops based there.

Among his many songs were ones about miracles ("It took a Miracle"), heaven ("Heaven Came Down"), and missions ("So Send I You"). His tunes about miracles might well have come from his real-life experiences—as a pilot in the war, when one of his engines shut down, or from a time prior to the war. The first miracle involved Peterson and his two brothers. Traveling from one concert to another—somewhere between Wichita, Kansas, and Lincoln, Nebraska—a semi-truck hit their car head on. Although the collision destroyed the car, the Peterson brothers walked away with only minor injuries.

So, as a kindergartner, I learned about worry from a man who knew how to combat it. While it was a simple song, it contained a powerful message: Why worry when you can pray?

It works, folks. It really works.

And yet, after many years of ministering to people, I know that worry is still one of their major causes of unrest, even among some strong Christians. While prayer is the answer, many remain in a worried state. Some even resort to ancient pagan rituals, like worry dolls, which take their name from the Mayan ancestors of Guatemalans. Rather than resorting to superstition, let's dive into this major cause of unrest and see what God can do.

Come to Me!

It always starts with Jesus. Christ devoted a fairly significant portion of His Sermon on the Mount to the worry issue. As defined today, worry is "to torment oneself with, or suffer from disturbing thoughts; fret;" and "to torment with cares, anxieties, etc.; trouble; plague."[2]

In Matthew 6:25-34, Jesus lists items people might worry about, such as food, drink, and clothing. In this passage, He reminds us that our heavenly Father already knows what we need, and if we seek Him, all these things will be added to us as well.

So, for all of you who think you are really advanced in thought and actions, who think you are socially aware, and connected with up to date issues, I remind you that worry is one of the oldest things in existence. Yet no other solution has ever been found that can measure up to this one: "Come to Me," says Jesus.

I recently saw an article online about the top things people worry about today. Although it featured twenty, the top ten will suffice. This survey of two thousand people showed that they worry most often about:

1. Getting old
2. Worried about my financial future
3. Low energy levels
4. My diet
5. Debt
6. Job security
7. Looking old
8. My physique
9. Paying my mortgage/rent
10. I seem to be generally unhappy[3]

Given these findings, it is pretty easy to see that things have not changed much in the last two thousand years. Logic will tell you that if our problems are the same as they were when Jesus walked on this earth, then the solution is also the same. For the skeptics who would say, "If the problems are still here, obviously the solution did not work," my response would be: "Oh, but it does work! I have tried it and found it to be true. And I know of many others who will testify to that truth."

Far too many people today are still worrying about the same things they did in the first century, whether that is about life in general, or what kind of —and how much—food they will eat, the clothes they will wear, or how they look. (By the way, how someone looks is the least-reliable barometer of what kind of a person they are or what they will be like to live with.) The saddest thing about the "worry habit" is that it takes far more energy than simply turning it all over to Jesus.

Remember, in Matthew 11:29 Jesus said that after we take on His yoke and learn from Him that "you will find rest for your souls." As I meditated on this passage, I thought about the power of God—the power with which Jesus operates. That launched me into additional study, especially of the Greek word translated as power: *dunamis*.

Here is what I found. *Dunamis* is not just any power, like the sports car that can go from zero to sixty in mere seconds or the explosive power of dynamite that can blow things up. This Greek root often refers to miraculous power or marvelous works (such as in Matthew 7:22, Mark 5:30, Luke 5:17, or Acts 8:13). According to Thayer's Greek-English Lexicon, it can also refer to "moral power and excellence of soul."[4]

"Perhaps most importantly, *dunamis* can refer to 'inherent power, power residing in a thing by virtue of its nature, or which a person or thing exerts and puts forth,'" says one Bible scholar. "In Matthew 22:29 Jesus tells the Sadducees, 'You are in error because you do not know the Scriptures or the *power* of God.' Jesus also said, 'Then will appear the sign of the Son of Man in heaven. And then all the peoples of the earth will mourn when they see the Son of Man coming on the clouds of heaven, with *power* and great glory' (Matthew 24:30). In other words, the Lord has inherent power residing in Himself. *Dunamis* is part of His nature."[5]

So, in the context of finding rest for your soul, think about the implication: *dunamis* can refer to excellence of soul. When Jesus says, "You will find rest for your soul," He is referring to the kind of power that He felt leave His body when the woman who desperately wanted healing reached out to touch His garment (you can read the full story in Matthew 9:20-23). Think of leading clairvoyants, fortune tellers, or mind readers who entertain audiences far and wide with their "skills"; none of them can feel power as it leaves their body to bring someone's healing. That is the kind of power and excellence of soul that is available to bring you rest!

No need to worry! God's "dunamis" (dynamite) power is available to us today.

STEP 2:

LET GO OF WEARINESS AND CARES

I suggest you make a list of all the things that are causing you worry. All the things that are keeping you awake at night, or that cloud your thinking, or that interrupt your thought processes during the day. Even without knowing you personally, I can predict that your list will not be much different than the survey results, or those Jesus mentioned. Once you have completed your list, pray about it. Try repeating a prayer that goes like this:

"Lord Jesus, I thank You that You have made a way for me to live worry free. As an act of faith, I am determining to seek first the kingdom of God and Your righteousness. Because I know that You have already made a way for me to live in the joy of your rest. Right now, I renounce and deny any power from (your list of worries) and determine to live my life in Your sufficiency."

Now take the list and do one of three things.

1. Tear it up and throw it away
2. Burn it
3. Bury it

In other words, totally let go!!!

STEP 3:
RECEIVE THE GIFT OF REST

You can claim this one from Philippians 4:6-7: "Be anxious for nothing, but in everything by prayer and supplication, with thanksgiving, let your requests be made known to God; and the peace of God, which surpasses all understanding, will guard your hearts and minds through Christ Jesus."

STEP 4:

LET JESUS BE YOUR PARTNER

I once pastored a church in Northern California. It was located in an urban area that allowed us to minister to many homeless individuals. I developed a relationship with one such couple. I am not sure if they were married, but they lived together and started attending our church. One day they invited me to their home: a tree that had a dense covering and low hanging limbs, which together provided some sense of privacy. They had even hung a chandelier from the branches that hung over their makeshift table: a small red cooler. No, the chandelier did not light up the house; there was no electricity. But it offered a semblance of home, and they were so glad they had a place to host their pastor.

Now, this couple seemed like a magnet for problems. The fact is, they were not a magnet for problems, but that is what I wanted to believe. The reality is they—the man in particular—constantly made poor lifestyle choices, such as abusing drugs and alcohol, stealing, and brawling. It was his lifestyle that brought the problems. To make matters worse, he was so lacking in confidence and self-esteem that bad decisions seemed to stalk him. While sitting in their living room under the tree (in the only chair they had, a low-slung beach number they had nabbed from a trash bin somewhere), I shared the love of Jesus with them. As I led them to profess faith in Christ, both of them cried and laughed. The thought went through my mind: "This must be the best day of their lives and one of the top ones for me as well."

In that moment, I thought about this man's unending series of bad choices. So, I also told them, "I want to help you. I want to be your partner in the future. And if you start down the wrong path again, I am going to reach out and pull you up." I stretched my arm and hand out in a motion of grabbing him by the hand and pulling him up.

So, what happened to that couple? I don't know. They soon disappeared from our midst. Gone with no forwarding address. I never saw them again. But here's my hope: that Jesus was living in their hearts! My hope is they found the real partner they needed, not me. I'm just a man. The real partner is the One who lives in their heart. He is the one who can carry the load.

He can carry your load of worries too. Have you made some bad choices in life? (And haven't we all?) No matter what you have done, He can handle that! Whatever issues you are struggling with, that's no problem for Him. Finances wrecked? Not only does He own it all, it is free to those who have received Him. He paid the bill in full on Calvary.

STEP 5:

LEARN FROM THE MASTER

In John 4, we read the fascinating story of Jesus and the woman at the well. She left home that morning with no idea that her entire life was about to change. She simply thought she would do what she likely did most every other day. She would go to the well, and at a time when she could be alone, so no one could judge her. After all, she had been married five times and was now living with a man who wasn't her husband (and you thought cohabitation was a modern invention). To her surprise, there was someone there that day who changed her life forever. Jesus spoke truth to her, but He did not condemn her. He knew her life story, in the same way He knows your life story. He knew of her sin, and He also knew that she could become a child of God. One redeemed with life everlasting.

So, what about your day? Are you just doing all the things you normally do? Are you avoiding something? Something that might speak of your own mistakes, or your own sin? Jesus wants to be your partner. He is so humble that even though He is God in the flesh, He invites us to share a yoke with Him. How awesome is that? He is not "lording" it over you, even though He is Lord of all. He is not judging you, even though He is the righteous Judge. In fact, He is "seeking" you. In the same way that He sought out the woman at the well, he is saying: "But the hour is coming, and now is, when the true worshipers will worship the Father in spirit and truth; for the Father is seeking such to worship Him" (John 4:23). All He wants is your worship, and He is worth it!

STEP 6:

PRACTICE REAL HUMILITY

I am aware that, for some people, worry is such an ever-present part of their life they would not know what to do if they could not worry. They would have nothing to talk about and nothing to complain about. Worry has been their companion for so long that it has become, in a rather strange way, a painful comfort.

It is time for some real humility. Confess that you are worrying about things that you cannot change, and that you need someone who can bear your load. Confess that you aren't smart enough to lighten your load, nor do you have the tools to make it happen. After all, our choices are very limited. We can continue to carry the load and suffer from a lack of sleep, poor concentration, deteriorating health, and so forth. Or, we can humbly submit to the Almighty God and receive His rest. Yes, it takes humility because you must admit: I can't do this alone.

STEP 7:

FIND TRUE PEACE OF MIND

Whenever worry becomes a stronghold in my mind, I immediately resort to the stanza that opened this chapter: "Why worry when you can pray? Trust Jesus, He'll be your stay."

With that in mind, try this prayer:

Thank you, Lord God Almighty, that I do not need to resort to my own stinkin' thinkin' and start worrying about my troubles. I am thankful I can rely on Your Word to be my stabilizer and a place of rest for my soul. Forgive me, Lord, for making worry more of a habit than following the discipline of trusting in Your promises. I worry too much, whether that involves financial worries or problems in my personal life, marriage, or family, or illness, or the past betrayal by a friend. There are so many storms around us: storms of materialism, storms of moral degeneracy, storms of injustice, and storms of terrorism and war. These are the kind of worries that plague my mind day in and day out.

Thankfully, the story of Christ's disciples on the Sea of Galilee in Mark 4 also gives my mind and body peace. He was at peace in the midst of a huge storm. Although His disciples panicked, He stayed fast asleep because He knew His Father God was in control. He knew You were sovereign over the storm, and that it would vanish at the word: "Peace, be still!" (v. 39). Your Word calmed the storm then and it calms my storms and worries today. It is Your Word that brings peace to my life.

You taught us in Romans 10:17 that faith comes by hearing Your Word proclaimed, so I speak Your words over my worries today. I rejoice that our Savior said, "In this world you will have tribulation; but be of good cheer, I have overcome the world" (John 16:33). I will say as the Psalmist did: "Your word I have hidden in my heart, that I might not sin against you" (Psalms 119:11).

Thank You, Father, that Your Spirit rests upon me—the same spirit as the "Rod from the stem of Jesse . . . the Spirit of wisdom and understanding, the Spirit of counsel and might, the Spirit of knowledge and of the fear of the LORD" (Isa. 11:1-2). I thank You for making me of quick understanding, and that my delight is in the obedient fear of You. I thank You for the ability to not judge by what I see or hear, but with the righteous judgment that comes from the Holy Spirit.

I choose to not worry as I live out my life in thankfulness to You. I thank You that all the benefits of Your words are mine. In the spirit of Psalm 1, I thank You that I do not live in the counsel of the ungodly or follow their advice, plans, and purposes. Nor do I stand, submissive or inactive, in the path where sinners walk. Nor do I sit down to relax and rest where the scornful and mockers gather. I delight in your law. I will continually meditate on it, ponder it, and study it day and night. I will "be like a tree planted by the rivers of water, that brings forth its fruit in its season, whose leaf also shall not wither; and whatever (I do) shall prosper" (Ps. 1:3).

Today, I will follow the advice of James 4:8 and draw close to you, Father, knowing that You will draw close to me. I have *no worries* because I believe the words of Psalm 91:11: For He shall give His angels charge over you, to keep you in all your ways." I will not spend my day worrying about what I did not accomplish yesterday or fearing what tomorrow will bring. I will "be anxious for nothing, but in everything by prayer and supplication, with thanksgiving, let (my) requests be made known to God" (Phil. 4:6). I will do this because Your Word has brought me peace. I will believe what the prophet Isaiah said: "All your children shall be taught by the LORD, and great shall be the peace of your children" (Isa. 54:13).

I will be a doer of the Word of God and blessed in my deeds. I will "incline (my) ear to (Your) sayings," knowing that "they are life to those who find them, and health to all their flesh." (Prov. 4:20 and 22). Like the Psalmist, "though I walk through the valley of the shadow of death, I will fear no evil; for You are with me; Your rod and Your staff, they comfort me" (Ps. 23:4).

Faith-filled words will become my servant, working for me day in and day out. I will do this by speaking things based on the authority of Your Word, God. Faith-filled words will be spiritual forces working on my behalf. They will get to my future before I do and prepare the way for me. You have taught me, Lord, through Your Word that I am framing my world daily by the words I am speaking. Therefore, I will not allow my spoken words to become idle and unproductive.

I choose to believe the words that our Savior spoke: "I say to you, whoever says to this mountain, 'Be removed and be cast into the sea,' and does not doubt in his heart, but believes that those things he says will be done, he will have whatever he says. Therefore I say to you, whatever things you ask when you pray, believe that you receive them, and you will have them" (Mark 11:23-24).

Amen and amen.

To that prayer, I would add one note:

WHY WORRY WHEN YOU CAN PRAY?!!!

CHAPTER 9
EXPRESSING ANGER

"Do not let the sun go down on your wrath."

~ Ephesians 4:26

Whoever thinks pastors are always full of smiles and joy whenever a newcomer visits their congregation hasn't encountered some of the unruly folks who show up periodically, like the woman who visited our church in California. My wife, Wilma, was trying to offer the woman help. But she shocked Wilma, suddenly taking some papers in her hand and swatting her as she shouted, "Why have you crossed your legs? Jesus would not do that!" (By the way, there wasn't a thing wrong with the way Wilma crossed her legs, but this woman could find fault with anyone—for any reason.)

As you might suspect, Wilma's words of encouragement fell on deaf ears. One time, that same woman called our house after midnight on New Year's Eve and asked, "How is my daughter doing?" I didn't know what she was talking about, until she told me that she had dropped her daughter off at our house at 11:00 that night. Since we weren't home at 11:00, I went outside to check. There, I found her twelve-year-old daughter asleep in the back seat of our car. Though, it was a cold night, the mother got angry at her daughter, so she dropped the girl off at our house. (I'm still not sure what she hoped to accomplish.) This lady was angry with her daughter, with Wilma, and—on more than one occasion—with me.

During this woman's battles with her own internal demons, her anger erupted at whoever happened to be closest at the moment. The positive element of this story: that woman initiated my education on demon possession, which in turn allowed me to offer constructive guidance and spiritual insights to many other people through the years.

ROOTS OF ANGER

Benjamin Franklin once said: "Anger is never without a reason, but seldom with a good one."[1] As I have, you have likely seen anger on display numerous times. Extreme, irrational, uncontrolled anger, the kind that is best described as rage. Yet the person who is seething with anger is typically fighting something on the inside that causes eruptions at the oddest and strangest of times. I have experienced such outbursts in the middle of corporate training sessions, or while counseling couples, or watching parents berate their kids. And, conversely, children screaming at their parents. In today's world, anger is freely and openly displayed against politicians, newscasters, sports figures, teachers, religious leaders . . . the list is nearly endless. It is not only an angry world in which we live, that anger is causing undue stress, anxiety, and even rioting and violence.

In addressing issues that cause unrest in our souls, I have looked at some factors causing tremendous anxiety on the inside. But anger is very different in its expression. Debt, fear, and worry are quiet enemies. When expressed in conversation (with some exceptions), they generally remain fairly calm. However, anger is more volatile, energized, and strident—more "in your face." While most of your stress may come from a quiet or even silent enemy, anger is so much more potent than fear or mental stress. Because of that, I often counsel people, "It wouldn't hurt to count to ten before you blow your stack." I am sure that many who lose their temper and vent steam publicly later feel bad about it.

What causes anger? William Penn—an English Quaker who later became the founder of Pennsylvania—once said that the person who is in the wrong is the first one to get angry. However, the truth is that what we see as anger is often unrelated to the moment, or the issue at hand. It is more likely something from yesterday, last week, or the distant past that suddenly bubbles to the surface and erupts in a rage so forceful it leaves many bystanders scratching their heads.

Now, not all anger is without justification. There is what I call "appropriate" anger: anger with a valid reason behind it, which needs to be demonstrated in an appropriate manner. Some of you are likely to remind me Jesus got angry before He tossed the money changers out of the temple (see Matthew 21:12). Yes, it appears that He did. That is a good example of anger appropriately demonstrated.

THE STEPS TO RESOLVING ANGER

In the same way I have reviewed steps to dealing with problems in several previous chapters, let's walk through the through the process Jesus provided in Matthew 11 for dealing with anger.

STEP 1:

COME TO ME

As I just mentioned, not all anger is sin. However, for the kind that is, only Jesus can take care of it. After all, it was sin that caused the Son of God to die on the cross. As Jesus bore our sin He said: "Father, forgive them, for they do not know what they do" (Luke 23:34). So, let's start by bringing it all to Jesus. To do so, you must admit, confess, and repent. I still remember an episode years ago, when a man stood before me with clenched fists, bulging veins in his neck, and face contorted while he fumed: "I am not angry!" We have all been there, right? Remember; admit, confess and repent to receive forgiveness for your sin.

LET GO OF WEARINESS AND CARES

As a pastor for many years, I regularly dealt with anger and its fallout. Though I have to be delicate about revealing any private, personal conversations, the following composite description reflects a typical conversation I had with a number of people from my congregations. Although they came to me for help dealing with anger issues, it soon became apparent they were holding onto something. Something they should have dealt with years earlier. Anger allowed to fester will affect your perspective on many other issues, which just compounds your problem.

The typical conversation would go like this:

I would ask a seemingly benign question like: "When did your anger issues first appear? Can you remember when you first realized how angry you are?" I did this in an effort to uncover the source of the anger.

"It all started with my divorce."

"How long ago was the divorce?" I replied.

"Five years ago."

"How many people have you talked to this week about your divorce?" I would ask.

"A few," she said.

"How many is a few?"

"Several," she replied.

"How many is several?"

"Six!"

"You know, if I were to talk to six people a week for five years about any negative thing in my life, I think I would feel like you do. And I know that I would not heal either. You need to let it go."

Thus, the solution: Let it go.

Let's face facts. How many things are you holding on to that still make you angry weeks, months, or—as I so often heard—years later? How long can you hold on to this anger? How long should you hold on to it? After dealing with it so many times over the years, I can confidently say: It is time to let it go. This is not an easy task. Anger is a strong emotion, and when you are emotional, you're not very rational! So, you need to cool down enough to think rationally and biblically about your anger.

God confronted Cain about his anger with a few simple questions: "Why are you angry? And why has your countenance fallen? If you do well, will you not be accepted?" (Gen. 4:6-7). Of course, an all-knowing God does not ask questions in order to gain information! God wasn't puzzled about Cain's anger or even upset by it. Instead, He wanted Cain to analyze it and admit the truth: he was jealous of his brother, who had offered his very best instead of trying (as

Cain did) to skate by giving a minimum effort. Today, God might ask you and me the same question: "Why are you angry?" The answer may lie in examining our faults, shortcomings, or self-centered actions in a particular situation. Or, by admitting how we contributed to contentiousness with another person. Sure, they may have crossed the line, but did you help push them there?

If you really want peace, and desire and need the rest that God is offering, you need to let go . . . now! I talked with a longtime friend just recently who had lost his wife to cancer more than two years ago. He has dealt with the grief better than most because he earnestly sought help from the Lord for his grief, studied Scripture, and practiced what he learned. When we chatted recently, he told me: "Last night I asked God, for the first time, to take away my anger."

He then related the painfully-forged insight that much of grief is related to anger, and how freeing it felt to ask the Lord for help. Now, if a mature man of faith had been carrying anger for months on end, and found help by asking the Lord to remove it, why not do the same?

STEP 3:

RECEIVE THE GIFT OF REST

There are ten mentions (in the New King James Version) of "rest" in the book of Hebrews. The first concludes

a passage where God talks about the steep price the Israel-
ites in the desert paid for their grumbling: "Therefore, as
the Holy Spirit says: 'Today, if you will hear His voice, do
not harden your hearts as in the rebellion, in the day of trial
in the wilderness, where your fathers tested Me, tried Me,
and saw My works forty years. Therefore I was angry with
that generation, and said, 'They always go astray in their
heart, and they have not known My ways.' So I swore in My
wrath, 'They shall not *enter My rest*'" (Heb. 3:7-11, emphasis
added). You may recognize verse 11 from its previous use in
chapter 3, also on this topic of rest.

The next chapter of Hebrews starts with: "Therefore,
since a promise remains of entering His rest, let us fear lest
any of you seem to have come short of it" (Heb. 4:1). So what
makes the difference? Why is there is a promise, but some
won't receive it? We can find the answer in Hebrews 3:12-13:
"Beware, brethren, lest there be in any of you an evil heart
of unbelief in departing from the living God; but exhort one
another daily, while it is called 'Today,' lest any of you be
hardened through the deceitfulness of sin." In other words,
the key to rest is faith. The barrier to rest is unbelief.

One recent morning, as I do every morning, I tuned
into the "GodToday" message that comes to my email from
GodTV. These brief, two-to-three minute encouragements
always speak to me. I have been soaking in Matthew 11:28-30
for weeks as I have been writing this book, and found myself
quite blessed by that day's message. Written by Bob Weiner

of Bob Weiner Ministries, it said in part:

"The Lord said, 'Your faith level, Bob, is not big enough to get the job done. Get your faith level up and your yoke will be easy and your burden will be light. And you will do more in one year than you have done in your whole life-time.' Ladies and gentlemen, the Lord loves faith. So, all we have to do is get our faith level up and the yoke will be easy and the burden will be light."

Do you see where he took me that day? Right to the words of Jesus in Matthew 11:30: "My yoke is easy and my burden is light." I'm taking you back there too. Lift your faith level up, and the yoke will be easy and the burden will be light.

STEP 4:

LET JESUS BE YOUR PARTNER

Remember the yoke; you and Jesus are in it together. Anger is such a strong emotion that many cannot handle it alone. That is why you will see "anger management classes," but not many "worry management" or "fear management" or "stress management" classes. Okay, I looked online and found some anxiety/worry classes, but not nearly as many as anger management. It's the more obvious issue.

My point here is that you need to partner with Jesus for total victory. Recently I heard about a young man who was yelling at a woman at the bus stop for "not treating me with respect." A man stepped in to protect the woman, and the young man started beating the older man with a folder that he was holding. Finally, he dropped the folder and ran away. After someone called the police, they were able to identify the offender because of the folder he dropped—it happened to contain the homework from his anger management class. Ok folks, truth be told, this is only a humorous tale, not a true story, but it still makes a point: If you rely on your own devices, you might well end up like that young man. With Jesus as your partner, you are much better-equipped to overcome inappropriate anger. You will also learn how, and when, to express a godly kind of anger.

STEP 5:

LEARN FROM THE MASTER

There are a lot of questions about anger stemming from the verse that opened this chapter. The full passage reads like this: "'Be angry, and do not sin'": do not let the sun go down on your wrath, nor give place to the devil" (Eph. 4:26-27).

There are times when anger is appropriate. When you hear of a man who is ruining his family because of sexual sin or his out-of-control anger, you should get angry. Getting angry at sin is justified. When you hear of someone who is causing problems in a church over petty issues or by spreading gossip, anger is the correct reaction. If you hear of a little child who is being abused, mistreated, or neglected, it should upset you as well. Anger is the proper response in each situation because it is God's response. Anger at sin is right! Still, we must be careful in how we process our anger. This passage tells us "Be angry" and then adds, "but do not sin." We would be wrong not to be angry in those situations, because apathy towards sin is not a godly response either.

So, when you are angry, you must determine whether it is righteous or unrighteous anger. Let me give you a helpful guideline: If you are to be angry and not sin, then you must be angry at nothing but sin!

During the years I spent as a pastor, there were certain things that made me very angry, particularly marital unfaithfulness. Learning that spouses were having affairs or sleeping around really bothered me, especially when it involves people proclaiming they follow Christ (whose teachings on marital fidelity are quite clear). As I look back, I think that particular sin—especially within church leadership—was such an issue because marriage is to reflect a picture of Christ and His church.

Ephesians 5:22-30 spells out how husbands are to love their wives in the same way "the Lord does the church" (v. 29). So, one time when I found out that one of our leaders was having an affair, I sat outside the house at 4:00 a.m. where he and the woman were having a rendezvous. I knew that he would be leaving in the early morning hours. When he came out . . . surprise!

On another occasion I knocked on the door where another leader was having an affair. When no one answered, I said loudly: "I know you are in there, and I am not leaving until you come out. And every thirty minutes I will knock again to remind you that I am here." This went on for several hours, until he finally came out. The results: three marriages were redeemed—both parties from the first account, and one marriage from the second account (in the latter, the female participant was single). My point: anger at sin can have a positive impact. Indeed, those married couples still thank me to this day.

Now, on the same topic, when it involved people who weren't involved in leadership, we used a much different approach. Why? Because of the admonition in James: "My brethren, let not many of you become teachers, knowing that we shall receive a stricter judgment" (James 3:1). So, for those in leadership we had a stricter method. With new Christians, non-Christians, or backslidden Christians, we approached them with God's love, compassion, and forgiveness. That, along with good counsel and teaching, is better than anger.

STEP 6:

PRACTICE REAL HUMILITY

Since anger is such a visible—and therefore public—emotion, you can cannot easily hide it. You might be able to hide your worry or even your fear, but when the issue is anger, everyone around you typically can see it. Therefore, when you deal with it, doing it in a public and humble way is necessary if it involved a public eruption. When the anger is public, so too should be the response.

How do you deal with a recent outburst of anger? Humility. That means no excuses, no justification, and no casting of blame on others. Own up to your mistake. As James 5:16 teaches, confess it so you can find healing.

STEP 7:

FIND TRUE PEACE OF MIND

Let me remind you again, public expressions of anger may need to be addressed publicly. For example, if you explode before a group of friends or fellow coworkers or in your church, it is a good idea to apologize to those who experienced (and may have been deeply wounded) by your anger. In addition to asking for their forgiveness, make a commitment to avoid acting that way in the future.

However, the root of your anger originated in your mind, which is where you must find victory. In a quiet place, spend time with the Lord and ask Him to help you deal with your anger. It doesn't have to be a public eruption; remember the friend I mentioned earlier who lost his wife to cancer and asked God to take away his anger? Even though it was a private, one-on-one sort of issue, he still needed to deal with it. Which he did with the simple prayer: "Lord, please take away my anger." Nothing profound there. Yet that represented two huge steps toward: 1) full release from the anger and 2) living free of it.

So, go ahead. The only thing you have to lose is the controlling, domineering emotion that keeps you locked up in a prison of bitterness. Pray this prayer:

Dear Father, I am realizing there is no way to live victorious apart from trusting You with my anger issues. I desire to consecrate my body, my behavior, my words, my thoughts, my attitudes, and motives to Your will. I let go of trying to live under my own control and roll it over to You. I submit my will to Your timing as You purify me so I can live and serve You more effectively.

Holy Spirit, I desire You to lead my thoughts and emotions into greater freedom and transparency of Your kingdom coming and Your will being done in my life. I want to know what is on Your heart concerning my destiny. Thank you, Lord, that by Your spirit I can "put off all these: anger, wrath, malice, blasphemy, filthy language" (Col. 3:8) from my lips. And, that I can follow the advice of Proverbs 15:18, which teaches that a hot-tempered man starts fights, but a patient man brings peace to a situation.

Help me to be quick to listen, slow to speak, and slow to become angry. I recognize that human anger does not bring about the kind of righteous life that You desire. I make that my desire too. Amen.

CHAPTER 10

THE FINAL STRESSORS

"Therefore if the Son makes you free,
you shall be free indeed."

~ John 8:36

P eople in general have a tendency to float from
one extreme to the other. It can be something as
complicated as a personality disorder or something
as simple as needing a cup of coffee. Over the years, I have
seen people in the church, business, and ministry environ-
ments make dramatic shifts of a spiritual nature. Although
perhaps not as serious in a practical sense, they still cause
damage. I'm talking about people who move from enjoying
God's grace to insisting that everyone follow the law (while
generally carving out an exception for themselves). Others
gravitate from freedom into bondage. Or, they revert from

stress-free living to trying to follow so many rules to relieve stress that they wind up manufacturing more of it.

In this book, I have sought to provide you with a template for dealing with many of life's stressors. While it is a biblical model introduced by Jesus, the author of freedom, I can easily envision some readers turning these guidelines into "new rules" by posing such questions as: "Well, how do I make sure I have done step 3?" "Can you make step 4 clearer?" "How can I be sure I've finished all seven steps?"

I'm not exaggerating. Once, during a church staff retreat, I watched several young staff members struggling to finish all their daily Bible readings on time; in order to meet some prescribed reading and memorization goals set by their team leader. Instead of enjoying spending time with God and getting direction from His Word, they reaped a mountain of stress. Meanwhile, the leader was pressuring his team to fulfill these daily tasks with the unspoken and yet still obvious intent: "This will make you more spiritual." I watched these young Christians striving so hard to please their boss that they made pleasing him equal with pleasing God (a habit he encouraged). As a result, something that should have been rewarding became a grueling, thankless drudgery that offered little enjoyment or fulfillment. A "retreat" became anything but for those unfortunate souls.

In her book, *To Live is Christ*, excellent Bible teacher Beth Moore says that "trying to know God and serve Him before we come to love Him is exhausting."[1] A friend and skilled business leader, Terry Tyson, puts it this way: "Fear, anxiety, and stress empower self-rule, meaning self sits on the throne and you try to manage problems by yourself. That is exhausting." Beth and Terry have arrived at the same conclusion: doing it yourself produces the opposite of rest.

So, I urge you to avoid making a template for entering God's rest an exercise in legalism. Trying to do things perfectly or check things off a list just so you can say you've done them misses the point entirely. It means trying to enter into rest could actually cause more stress!

Ironically, that is the way the world often sees Christ's followers. We have so many rules, so many things you "cannot do," and so many structures and game plans that are hard—if not impossible—to live up to . . . well, can you blame those outside the church if they want no part of this kind of life? I can't help but feel that even Christians who set these unrealistic expectations want out themselves. After all, they have built a room with no doors or windows. There is no way of escape.

German monk Martin Luther, whose protest of Catholic Church practices in the early 1500s sparked the Protestant Reformation, once said: "Thus, dear friends, I have said it clearly enough, and I believe you ought to understand it and not make liberty a law."[2] Within these pages I am offering a template, not a rule or a law. *God@Rest* is *not the exclusive way* to find rest. Indeed, if it becomes any of these things we have both wasted our time.

At the same time, it is a plan that Jesus offered, and what He offers is always free. He paid the price for your sins on the cross at Calvary so that salvation became a gift, not something you can earn. Reach out in faith and receive it. He has also already done all that is needed for you to enter into His rest. It is the kind of lasting rest that He offers everyone who trusts in Him. After all, no other living creature can boast that His works "were finished from the foundation of the world" (Heb. 4:3).

Since Jesus purchased your salvation through His sacrifice, that is all you need to enter into God's rest! The ability to live a stress-free, worry-free life has been finished from the beginning of time. God, the all-knowing, all-powerful, and omniscient Lord, knew exactly what you would need to live in a frenetic, fast-paced, all-consuming, chaotic twenty-first century and has already provided it for you. So, step in, receive it, and walk in liberty.

With that said, I think it is worthwhile reviewing a few more stressors—the robbers of rest. If we want real peace of mind; we need to enter into such a close relationship with the giver of peace that finding peace is not a drudgery in itself. So as we near the end of the book, I want to also discuss a few more of the enemy's tools that rob us of our rest; so let's take a quick look at guilt, shame, and lust. Obviously this is not an all-inclusive list, but hopefully it will give you the faith to believe that "with God all things are possible" (Matt. 19:26).

• GUILT

With each obstacle, the answer starts the same way: come to Jesus. I have often said that guilt is a tool of Satan that he tries to use to keep you in bondage. On the other hand, conviction is a tool of God to bring you to freedom and a powerful, Spirit-led and Spirit-controlled life. If you focus exclusively on the guilt, you will continue to feel burdened and slog through life with the mindset of: "I always do it wrong; I always fail; I will never succeed."

The cure is to allow the Lord to deal with your guilt. That tug in your heart right now is not a message from the Lord, proclaiming how disappointed He is in you. No, that tug is His conviction, urging you to face the problem and deal with it. The true measure of conviction is confessing what you have done wrong and turning away from it. Those steps will lead to thanksgiving for God's forgiveness and God-led inspiration to live right!

I recognize some folks who are reading this may have a tough time receiving this gift of grace. It may help to meditate on the theology behind grace. Recently, the excellent Bible teacher Andrew Wommack, the founder of Charis Bible College, shared some of the most insightful comments about grace I have ever heard. He said in part:

"The sad thing is God is the most misunderstood, misrepresented, most maligned person that has ever existed. Satan and religion have gone out of their way to misrepresent God. Some of it has been taken from the Bible. I know that may shock people, but there are parts of the Bible where the wrath of God was poured out in a very judgmental, punishing way. People don't understand that the new covenant is just that. A new covenant. A new contract. We have been set free. God has not changed, but what He did was take the judgment for our sins and put it upon Jesus. Because He has now punished His own Son He is now just and righteous to forgive us over things that in the old covenant there was no forgiveness, there was just punishment.

"God is not this harsh, angry God that is leaning over the banister of heaven with a lightning bolt, just ready to get you when something goes wrong. God punished His own Son. Today there is love and acceptance towards anyone who has received Jesus as their personal Lord. So, the nature of God does not change. But, the way He deals with us changed. According to the word of God in 1 John 4:8, 'God is love.' That is His true nature. He loves you today more than you have ever recognized."

When you understand that love and forgiveness; just receive it. No need to beg and plead; you know that He has provided a way. Remember, as Hebrews 4:3 says, "His works were finished from the foundation of the world".

You don't need to follow the prescribed "7 Steps to Rest" or spend the next three months in an advanced education course. Just accept His promise, right now. As the prophet Balaam spoke long ago: "God is not a man, that He should lie, nor a son of man, that He should repent. Has He said, and will He not do? Or has He spoken, and will He not make it good?" (Num. 23:19). He is the strong One; He can carry the load. You are not alone. His purity and blood are covering your sin. A simple solution is to let your prayers become a two-way conversation. Instead of talking constantly as you pray, stop periodically and listen. He has a lot to say.

It crosses my mind that one way prayers; prayers where we do all the talking and little listening is built upon a very self-promoting theology. And possibly even a theology full of doubt in the power of God that causes us to replace God's grace with our own ability to impress both God and those that might hear our eloquent words. So remember that Scripture says: "God resists the proud, but gives grace to the humble" (1 Pet. 5:5). In Matthew 11:28-30, Jesus taught us that "His yoke is easy" because He is well able to carry the load, and "His burden is light" because what might be heavy to us is light to Him.

When your mind is fully focused on Him; and when your faith is strong; guilt is dealt with in a simple prayer: "Thank you Jesus! My sin is forgiven and I am guilt free!"

- **SHAME**

In my experience, one of life's most debilitating stressors is shame. It affects the way you look, the way you feel, and the way you approach your daily existence. The Word offers a welcome counterbalance, especially the Psalm that says: "They looked to Him and were radiant, and their faces were not ashamed" (Ps. 34:5). The Psalmist understood how to face down shame.

Another translation phrases the Psalm this way: "Those who look to him for help will be radiant with joy; no shadow of shame will darken their faces" (Ps. 34:5 NLT). When you look at Jesus, you will only see love. When you look into His eyes, you will only see forgiveness. In His presence all shame is gone.

When you were a child, and even as an adult—maybe just yesterday or today—someone said, "Shame on you." They did not like something you had done, and were judging (cursing?) you with shame. A well-meaning (or maybe not so well-meaning) friend can offer condemnation for your actions with the familiar phrase: "Shame on you." Here is the difference between Jesus and the world: When He sees you do something that is wrong, He offers forgiveness. Why? Because He loves you and has already done all that needs to be done to take away your shame.

Let's make an agreement right now to never again say, "Shame on you" to another person. And, to never again accept the negative impact of those words when someone might say them to you. A loving God does not utter those words. He takes the shame—even the shadow of it—off your face. You can walk through with your head held high and the confidence of a loving and forgiving God on your side. Receive the promise of "no shame."

That's it. Just accept it.

When someone wants to curse you with shame, just look to your side. There stands Jesus, the shame taker! You are free.

Those who look to Him for help will radiate with joy; no shadow of shame will darken their faces. As the Bible teaches: "Everyone who believes in him will not be put to shame" (Rom. 10:11).

The One whose teaching forms the template for this book is the most powerful presence in the world, and yet He is still humble.

So pray with a thankful heart that shame is gone. In its place, humility has come. Remember Christ's yoke is easy and light.

All right! One more, and it is a biggie. Yes, there are many more issues that can and do cause us to lose control of our minds. I am not trying to review all of them, but to give you solid principles that you can use to conquer all of them. And so the final one for now is:

• LUST

The Bible has numerous warnings about lust. For example, Proverbs warns men to avoid an evil temptress: "Do not lust after her beauty in your heart, nor let her allure you with her eyelids" (Prov. 6:25). Paul urged the Romans: "Let us walk properly, as in the day, not in revelry and drunkenness, not in lewdness and lust, not in strife and envy" (Rom. 13:13). I John talks about lust that can come through our flesh, eyes, or life's pride, and declares this "is not of the Father but is of the world. And the world is passing away, and the lust of it" (I John 2:16-17).

To turn to a practical definition, the entry on lust from the familiar online source, Wikipedia, begins: "Lust is a craving; it can take any form such as the lust for sexuality, lust for money or the lust for power. It can take such mundane forms as the lust for food as distinct from the need for food. Lust is a psychological force producing intense wanting for an object, or circumstance fulfilling the emotion."[4]

In other words, lust is a force that consumes the mind; and there is nothing mundane about it, no matter what the above definition says. It can be so strong that it allows little or nothing else in, which ultimately controls more than the mind. It also governs the actions that flow from the constant attention the mind devotes to it. More often than not, it is a lust for sex, especially the desire for someone other than your marriage partner.

Jesus warned against using the eyes for unhealthy purposes. Right after He advised people to lay up treasures in heaven instead of craving earthly riches, He said, "The lamp of the body is the eye. If therefore your eye is good, your whole body will be full of light. But if your eye is bad, your whole body will be full of darkness. If therefore the light that is in you is darkness, how great is that darkness!" (Matt. 6:22-23).

The point here is that the eyes and lust are closely connected. Jesus wants you to deal with whatever has come into your mind through the eyes. So, if looking (with lust) is an issue for you—and it is for millions—let us deal with it right now. I again invite you to come to Jesus with your lust. Does that strike you as embarrassing and too "private" an issue to deal with? Get over it; He already knows. You have not hidden anything from Him. You may fool your spouse, and you may fool your friends, and you may even think you have fooled yourself. But Jesus knows!

In this case (and in every other case as well, but especially with lust), it is very important for you to be honest with the Lord. Remember, He already knows, so let Him know that you are also aware of how much damage lust is doing to you. Lay it out in prayer with an earnest desire and request for release.

You may not feel weary with your lust. In fact, it may even energize you—toward taking the wrong action. But, as it has with numerous political figures, entertainers, and even church leaders, the weight of this issue will bring you down if you don't deal with it. Numbers 32:23 promises that you can "be sure your sins will find you out." Almost every week we read of another leader whose sexual lust has been revealed to the entire world, and with consequences far costlier than if they had dealt with it privately. They all mistakenly thought they could get by with it. Even if you could, God still knows. So, let it go.

God is offering a gift for your soul. So much of lust is giving into the pleasure of the moment with little thought for the future. But when God offers His rest; the offer is for peace of mind today, and eternal life for your future. What an offer!

It has been proven over and over again; that most of us are not strong enough to handle lust with just sheer will power. You (and I) need to get in the yoke with Jesus and let Him carry the load. He is the ultimate overcomer. You need Him to relieve the burden of lust and help you resolve it for good.

In early March of 2018, my wife and I sat and watched the telecast of the funeral of longtime evangelist Billy Graham. We cried, sang along with the old hymns, and rejoiced over the life of this man of God. Had he lived another eight months, he would have reached the century mark. Yet, thanks to some wise guidelines he and members of his evangelism team established decades earlier, he was able to avoid the scandals that have plagued so many. Still, while Billy Graham was an awesome servant of the Lord, he was not perfect. Only Jesus holds that title—and He is offering to be your teacher! The only holy, pure, righteous, and sinless Man to have ever lived is saying, "Learn from Me."

It takes humility to confess your wrongdoing, admit your faults, and come clean about your failures. But Jesus understands that. No matter how hard it seems to you, remember with Christ it is easy and light. That is the promise of Matthew 11:30. Because it came from Jesus, you can rely on it. As the old saying goes, you can "take it to the bank."

THE FINAL RESOLUTION

Now, whether you are struggling with guilt, shame, or lust—or all three—the best way to overcome them is by taking the situation to God. Here is a suggested prayer:

Prayer for release from guilt, shame, or lust

Lord, Romans 12:2 says, "Do not be conformed any longer to this world, but be *transformed* by the renewing of your mind." I desire Your transformation of my mind. As your Word teaches, faith comes by hearing your Word and declaring it. So may this transformation come through declaring and speaking what You say about me and my situation.

I will speak Your Word by faith so it can penetrate the darkness in my life. I thank you, Lord, that You will not let me be put to shame, nor let those who mock me triumph over me. In You I will put my trust. I praise Your name that in You, and in You alone, there is deliverance from guilt, shame, and lust.

No one whose hope is in You will ever be put to shame. Therefore, I hold fast to Your statutes and will speak of Your statutes to those You put in my path. I will not be put to shame. My salvation and my honor depend on You my God: You are my mighty rock and refuge. You will increase my honor and comfort me once again. As Your Word says: "Behold, I lay in Zion a stone for a foundation, a tried stone, a precious cornerstone, a sure foundation" (Isa. 28:16); it also promises that those who trust in Him will never be put to shame.

May Your favor rest on me, my Lord and God, and establish the work of my hands. I pray that I might fully understand your love and grace as I receive the favor that You have for my life, for I know that without Your favor the ways of the unfaithful are hard.

I thank you Lord that in You I can take refuge. Thank you for my deliverance into Your righteousness. I choose to live in the authority of the Word, for Your Word is creative and powerful. I receive Your transformation in my life.

In the name of the Lord Jesus, Amen.

FINAL NOTES

I wrote this book for those who really want help. Namely, those who are tired of rules, regulations, or "to do" lists. So please, do yourself a favor and look at the templates, outlines, and prayers you just reviewed as examples instead of as another set of directives that you *must* follow. That said, these templates are powerful and will work for you if you use them. Just do so in a spirit of joyful cooperation with God, not as trying to follow a legalistic set of obligations.

If you want to see some changes in your life (and who doesn't?), try memorizing this book's key passage, Matthew 11:28-30. It is easy to follow the seven steps if you simply apply this scripture to each cause of stress in your life. Memorizing it will make it easier to recall and implement in the midst of daily challenges. As you are able to do so, you may become a hero of sorts to others. Not because you're so great, but because you will have a quick and ready, scripturally-based answer to many of life's troublesome situations.

And, although I know that I should not have to say this . . . I will anyway. You can use this template for almost any challenge in life. While I chose to review some of what I consider the big ones, they may not be so big for you. That doesn't matter, because all of us deal with some formidable obstacles in life. You can use the same principle for almost any of the issues that cause us to lose our personal drive and stumble through our days with exhaustion, frustration, and unrest.

Imagine with me a life where you have constant peace of mind! A life without stress. A life full of energy. A life full of purpose. Can you imagine all the work that will get done, and all the wasted hours turned productive? Do me a favor. If this works for you, tell a friend. And, if you would, let me know as well.

~ Rich Marshall, rich@Godisworking.com

FOOTNOTES

INTRODUCTION

1. Tanya Mohn Forbes February 28, 2014

CHAPTER 1: FINDING A LASTING REST

1. You can find more background about the genesis and purposes of the Seven Mountains movement on pages 130-132 of *God@Work II*.

CHAPTER 2: ENTERING GOD'S REST

1. Kimberly Amadeo, "Haiti Earthquake: Facts, Damage, Effects on Economy," updated August 26, 2017, https://www.thebalance.com/haiti-earthquake-facts-damage-effects-on-economy-3305660.
2. Rich Marshall, *God@Work*, Volume 2: Developing Ministers in the Marketplace (Shippensburg, PA: Destiny Image Publishers, 2005), 26.

CHAPTER 4: REST FOR PEAK PERFORMANCE

1. Jim Loehr and Tony Schwartz, "The Making of a Corporate Athlete," *Harvard Business Review,* January 2001, https://hbr.org/2001/01/the-making-of-a-corporate-athlete.
2. Ibid.
3. Christina Hamlett, "How Stress Affects Your Work Performance," Chron, http://smallbusiness.chron.com/stress-affects-work-performance-18040.html.
4. Jungwee Park, "Work stress and job performance," *Perspectives,* December 2007, 5-17, http://statcan.gc.ca/pub/75-001-x/2007112/article/10466-eng.pdf.
5. E.J. Mundell, "Antidepressant use in U.S. soars by 65 percent in 15 years," *Healthday,* August 16, 2017, https://www.cbsnews.com/news/antidepressant-use-soars-65-percent-in-15-years/.

CHAPTER 5: PRACTICAL GUIDE TO REST

1. Rich Marshall, *God@Work: Discovering the Anointing for Business* (Shippensburg, PA: Destiny Image Publishers, 2000), xiii.
2. Ibid., 57.
3. Ibid., 99.
4. Dictionary.com, "passion," http://www.dictionary.com/browse/passion.

CHAPTER 8: WHY WORRY WHEN YOU CAN PRAY?

1. John W. Peterson, "Why Worry When You Can Pray?" Lyrics used by permission of John W. Peterson Music.

2. From Dictionary.com, http://www.dictionary.com/browse/worry?s=t.

3. "The 20 things people worry about the most," https://www.indy100.com/article/the-20-things-people-worry-about-the-most--xJVjF0DSox.

4. Joseph Thayer, Thayer's Greek-English Lexicon of the New Testament, (Peabody, MA: Hendrickson Bible Publishers, 1995), citation taken from S. Michael Houdmann, President, GotQuestions.org, https://www.gotquestions.org/dunamis-meaning.html.

5. Ibid.

CHAPTER 9: EXPRESSING ANGER

1. BrainyQuote®, Benjamin Franklin quotes, https://www.brainyquote.com/quotes/benjamin_franklin_382924.

CHAPTER 10: THE FINAL STRESSORS

1. GoodReads, "To Live is Christ Quotes," https://www.goodreads.com/work/quotes/251325-to-live-is-christ-embracing-the-passion-of-paul.

2. GoodReads, "Martin Luther Quotes," https://www.goodreads.com/quotes/246067-thus-dear-friends-i-have-said-it-clearly-enough-and.

3. From "GodToday" program on GodTV, March 2, 2018.

4. Wikipedia, "Lust," https://en.wikipedia.org/wiki/Lust.

51067187R10096

Made in the USA
Middletown, DE
29 June 2019